PRAIS[...]

"Jon Wells is the bes[...] His books are without riv[...] e human tragedy. He is a star in the genre. His books read like novels but are rich in true crime details, and his intimate look at the horrific crimes are woven with a human touch that hooks the reader from page one."

> —Sue Sgambati, veteran TV crime reporter and journalist

### Poison

"A riveting piece of crime reporting... a contemporary journey into a true heart of darkness."

> —Jerry Todd-Jenkins, *Canada Post* (U.K.)

"Intrepid reporter Jon Wells follows the marathon investigation and subsequent judicial proceedings from Canadian courtrooms to the baking streets of the Punjab, focusing on the personalities involved in this true international drama."

> —Alex Good, *The Record* (Kitchener-Waterloo, Ontario)

### Sniper

"[*Sniper*]dips into the snake pit of James Kopp's mind, a very scary place."

> —Duncan McMonagle, *Winnipeg Free Press*

"*Sniper* is an unsettling but enthralling journey into the lives and psyches of Kopp and his associates. Unsettling, because it deals with a kind of domestic terrorism, deep conviction that turns into criminality. Enthralling, because it's a well-told psychological detective story."

> —Mary Nesbitt, Managing Director, Readership Institute, Northwestern University, Illinois

"In *Sniper*, Wells will walk you through the mind of a killer with his edge-of-your-seat style of journalism. Excellent book for true crime lovers ....Without a doubt, this gets a five out of five rating from me. Awesome!"
—Judith Kaye, "J. Kaye's Book Blog"

"Riveting ... engrossing ... Dedicated to journalistic integrity, Wells sticks to the court record, its filings and his extensive interviews with investigators, prosecutors, defense counsel and Kopp's aiders and the witnesses in this international manhunt. That this book was authored by a Canadian journalist adhering to the record and eschewing the polemics of this horrific crime and the politics of abortion captivates the reader for its unbiased commitment to the highest journalistic standards."
—John E. Drury, Washington D.C. (Amazon.com)

"An excellent, true crime page-turner."
—*The Guelph Mercury*

### Post-Mortem
"Fascinating....Wells spins out the story in novelistic form with richly detailed portraits of the main players... Meticulous, good old-fashioned story-telling. Jon Wells is a treasure who deserves recognition on the national literary stage.
—Chuck Howitt, *The Record*

# VANISHED

## COLD-BLOODED MURDER
## IN STEELTOWN

# JON WELLS

John Wiley & Sons Canada, Ltd.

*Library and Archives Canada Cataloguing in Publication Data*

Wells, Jon
        Vanished : cold-blooded murder in Steeltown / Jon Wells.

ISBN 978-0-470-15549-3

        1. Pirrera, Sam.  2. Murder—Investigation—Ontario—Hamilton.
3. Murderers—Ontario—Hamilton—Biography.  I. Title.

HV6535.C33H35 2009a        364.152'30971352        C2009-902924-3

**Production Credits**
Cover design: Ian Koo
Interior text design: Mike Chan
Typesetter: Natalia Burobina
Printer: Tri-Graphic Printing Ltd.

John Wiley & Sons Canada, Ltd.
6045 Freemont Blvd.
Mississauga, Ontario
L5R 4J3

Printed in Canada

1 2 3 4 5 TRI 13 12 11 10 09

**NEW LEAF PAPER®**
ENVIRONMENTAL BENEFITS STATEMENT
*of using post-consumer waste fiber vs. virgin fiber*

John Wiley & Sons - Canada saved the following resources by using New Leaf Pioneer, made with 100% post-consumer waste and processed chlorine free:

| trees | water | energy | solid waste | greenhouse gases |
|---|---|---|---|---|
| 24 fully grown | 10,349 gallons | 17 million Btu | 1,154 pounds | 2,274 pounds |

Calculations based on research by Environmental Defense Fund and other members of the Paper Task Force.

www.newleafpaper.com

ANCIENT FOREST FRIENDLY™

*For Ashlee*

# TABLE OF CONTENTS

# Preface

While making the rounds for media interviews for my true crime books, which have included true stories about a serial poisoner, doctor sniper, and bludgeoning husband, I have been asked more than once: *Doesn't this stuff get to you?* I reply that it surely would if not for the fact that I write in other genres, for example in my book *Heat* and in my writing for *The Hamilton Spectator*, where I don't cover the crime beat but venture into a variety of subject areas, from politics to sports and the arts. When I do visit the world of crime, I do so for relatively short, if intense, periods of time. Also, there are elements in the writing of true crime stories that keep me coming back, such as striving to give a voice to victims, bring them back to life on the pages. They also offer the chance to write about justice, both the legal and poetic variety, and to search for a measure of redemption in even the ugliest of tales.

*Vanished* was one book, however, that challenged me more than the others. I first read of the case of Sam Pirrera and his victims in the pages of the *Spectator* when my colleagues covered the story as it broke in 1999. But it wasn't until several years later that the notion of writing a book about the entire story came to me, when I was researching my book *Post-Mortem* and met with a Hamilton Police forensic detective named Gary Zwicker. "Special Agent Zwicker," as he playfully calls himself, is a character. As I prodded him for details about his life and career, he had that knowing grin on his face. "You're doing the ol' pregnant pause thing there—waiting for me to fill the space," he said. Zwicker had worked many nasty crime scenes, combing through them inch by inch, and I asked him what the worst thing was he had ever seen. His answer? The Pirrera case. He suggested that I might take it on as my next project.

I do not enter into these journalistic journeys lightly, however, and I wondered if it might be too dark a story to write. Instead I wrote a well-received series in the *Spectator* called "Emergency" about life and death in the ER of Hamilton General Hospital. Then (inevitably, I suppose) I pitched several ideas to my editor-in-chief, Dana Robbins, and I included among them a series on Pirrera, half hoping he would pass on it. But Dana suggested I tackle the case that shocked even veteran homicide investigators.

I interviewed uniformed Hamilton Police officers, detectives and a forensic pathologist who worked the case, often repeatedly, as well as a criminal profiler. I combed through court documents, search warrants, and interview transcripts, and studied crime scene and autopsy photos. I also met with family members and friends of the victims. As with all of my books I have written this story in a novelistic style, but every bit of detail, dialogue, and color comes directly from information gathered in interviews, documents, and direct observation. As in *Post-Mortem*, photographer Gary Yokoyama's considerable talent is again on display, illustrating scenes and characters from the story.

Returning to the question of whether this stuff ever gets to me, for reasons that will become clear, *Vanished* was as difficult a story to immerse myself in as any I have ever done; one that was not easy to keep on my desk and out of my head when the lights went out, not after all I had seen and heard. Looking back, perhaps that is why I began the narrative with a prayer. As for the search for redemption, I held out little hope of finding it after walking Sam Pirrera's dark and bloody path. It was in new research for the book that I found that redemption, just a glimpse. And in this story, even a mere glimpse is a considerable blessing.

*Jon Wells*
Hamilton, Ontario

# Acknowledgments

As always I thank Don Loney, Executive Editor at John Wiley & Sons, for making this book possible and for his suggestions and enthusiasm. At *The Hamilton Spectator*, I want to thank senior editor Cheryl Stepan for overseeing my work on the original series that appeared in the *Spectator*, which was then titled *To The Grave*, and Douglas Haggo, for yet again bringing his keen eye to copy editing the story. My colleague Carmelina Prete was one of the first reporters to cover the Pirrera case and, for the book, she helped me conduct an interview and provide feedback on drafts. It was a joy once again to work with photographer Gary Yokoyama who, typically, captured the tone of the story perfectly in his moody images. I thank Dana Robbins for his motivation and support, and also my former editor Roger Gillespie, who has long been a source of wisdom and friendship.

I thank officers with the Hamilton Police Service for their cooperation in my research after being initially and understandably reluctant to discuss it at all. I write about all of these officers by name in the story, but I single out assistance from forensic detectives Gary Zwicker and Ross Wood, and especially lead homicide investigator Peter Abi-Rashed. As always, most of all I thank family and friends of the victims for talking to me. I did not at all look forward to approaching family members to ask them to relive their anguish, even though as a writer I needed to hear it. They are brave people carrying unspeakable burdens; I thank them for letting me into their homes and lives. When I first met them, I said that this would be a dark story but that, on the positive side, I would try to shed some light on the lives of their loved ones and who they had been. If I have to some extent accomplished that, and if they felt a flicker of comfort from that, then it was all worth it.

# Chapter 1 ~ "You're Not Going Anywhere"

*Spring 1999*
*Gage Park*
*Hamilton, Ontario*

"Our Father, who art in heaven, hallowed be Thy name. Thy kingdom come, Thy will be done, on earth as it is in heaven."

A woman spoke the words under an eternal blue sky, sun shining, the air bone dry, a perfect day in the early spring of 1999, a day that otherwise might have offered a chance to contemplate renewal, rebirth, the annual deliverance from winter's grip. It had been an unusual and jarring winter, the weather shifting between extremes. A warm December had caused flowers to bloom incongruously, snapdragons poked up their heads. A month later, winter erupted with a fury that lasted just two weeks. Tundra swans flew through the city in March, as spring arrived early.

A dozen or so people gathered for the informal memorial service in Gage Park, wedged in the rugged and worn heart of the lower city. They had all known the victim, although most did not know her well. She had once lived just a few blocks away. They stood near the children's play area holding hands. The woman who organized it figured everyone there would know the words to the prayer, the one they all used to recite in classrooms when they were kids.

"Give us this day our daily bread, and forgive us our trespasses, as we forgive those who trespass against us."

Kids played on the swings. Plainclothes Hamilton police officers stood at a respectful distance from the gathering. In one sense, the nightmare was over. In another, it was just beginning. The epilogue would be little better than the bloody and unspeakable end.

"Lead us not into temptation. But deliver us from evil. For Thine is the kingdom, the power and the glory, forever and ever.

"Amen."

\* \* \*

*Easter weekend*
*Saturday, April 3, 1999*
*12 Burns Place, Hamilton*

He grabbed another dish. Smash. And another. Smash. Pieces littering the kitchen floor, plates, bowls. Smash. Smash. The cupboard bare. And now the furniture, baseball bat in his hands, slamming it into chairs, legs splintering, a mirror shattered. He had done this at times over the years, his anger exploding in a red-black fury, raging. He was unraveling, "decompensating" as psychologists put it, unable to keep his head when faced with acute stress—like the time he huddled alone, behind a trap door in the attic upstairs in his house, in the crawl space among the roof insulation, hiding from his dark past, present and future.

Saturday afternoon on Easter weekend he lay on the couch in his living room, his body quivering, curled into a fetal position.

*You think you're the one to tame me.*
*I'm your mother's worst nightmare*
*An out of control freak/Just wait and see*

He had been listening to the driving rhythms and violent lyrics of an Alannah Myles song, over and over and over again.

*I'm bad for you; I'll hurt your pride.*
*I'll put a hole in your heart*
*Ten foot wide; I make you feel*
*Like you wanna die.*

The anger had lived in him for a long time, but he had also shown control, had kept it together, his secrets not merely tucked away but burned forever. He made sure of that. But now he was coming apart at the seams, out of his comfort zone. And yet, with everything he had done, everything he was feeling, all that ripped at his insides, even as he was losing it, the stone cold would not leave him entirely. He had come this far. Get rid of it. Get rid of the body.

*I'm bad for you. I'll skin your hide.*
*What you're left with*
*You won't recognize.*
*If you run away now you'd be wise*
*Even I'd run from me if I could.*

The woman's last breath had come right there, in that house, his home, in the basement. She had wanted to leave the house on Burns Place, get away from him. She was just like the others. Women, he said, "They keep f----n' leaving me."

*You think you know all about me*
*'Cause you spent the night.*
*Yeah right, not quite.*

She told him she wanted to go.

*Keep f----n' leaving me.*

"You're not going anywhere," he said.

\* \* \*

Rookie Hamilton Police Constable Kathy Stewart pulled the cruiser into a variety store on Upper Wellington at Brucedale. It was early evening, Saturday, April 3. She was working an

8 a.m. to 8 p.m. shift on Easter weekend. She had just finished a sparse brown-bag lunch at the old Mountain police station, the building that had all the charm of an elementary school portable. A new station would soon be finished farther south on Hamilton Mountain off Rymal Road.

She felt a bit guilty about the junk food, but the bag of Doritos and bottled water would help address the growling in her stomach. She lived with her husband in a town nearby called Selkirk. When she married, she changed her name from her maiden Czemerynski, which saved her fellow officers the challenge of wrestling with the pronunciation.

It had been a grey day. Started off cool, then abruptly warmed, the sun showing itself in glimpses. By late afternoon the air was heavy and wet with a gathering storm. Stewart had done a park-and-walk at the Mountain Plaza. Wrote some parking tickets. The holiday weekend was always ripe for people leaving their cars where they shouldn't. And now she pulled away from the convenience store. Before she could open the Doritos a call came in on the mobile data terminal. It was 5:44 p.m.

Back then the MDTs were narrow message display centers, the cruisers not yet equipped with laptop-size screens. She pulled over to read a cryptic message: "Suspicious circumstances. 12 Burns Place."

She scrolled down further in the message. It said to check it out, and not to broadcast the call over the air. Call in if you need another unit for backup. Stewart typed a reply: "If the hairs on the back of my neck start tingling, I'll call you." She turned the cruiser east onto Concession Street and headed to the call.

Kathy Stewart might not have been working that day. She had almost switched with a rookie colleague. But here she was, and today was just her fifth solo shift on the job. She had always wanted to be a police officer. She was a big fan of the original *Law & Order* TV show, hungrily devoured mystery novels by writers like Patricia Cornwell and James Patterson. She was an athletic teenager, played basketball. But when she first applied to the Hamilton Police Service she didn't make the cut. Missed the mile-and-a-half distance run standard by about a minute. She attended Brock University, took a biology course in first year, when she was thinking of pursuing a career in physical education. Dissected pigs, cats. Ultimately she pursued law, got a law clerk qualification, ended up working in Toronto as a paralegal.

After six years in Toronto, she was 30 years old and ready to chase the dream again, serve her home community. She applied for Hamilton Police, trained hard for the run—a standard that is no longer used to determine eligibility to work as a cop—and this time nailed it. She was hired on September 1, 1998.

The long road to uniform was probably a good thing, she came to realize. Gaining life experience helps you deal with things you'll see and do on the job that might shake a younger person. Three months training at police college, and then assigned a beat on the Mountain, the ridge of limestone that stood from the last ice age and offered a bird's eye view of Hamiton's lower city, Big Steel's smokestacks, and Lake Ontario. Nothing ever happens on the Mountain, cops joked about the beat. It lacked the grit of old Hamilton, was known more for malls and conventional suburbia. Some domestics. Nothing major.

Stewart didn't hit the flashers or speed en route to 12 Burns Place. The call might amount to nothing. Dispatch had said a woman who called police would be waiting for her outside the house. There was no immediate emergency. At 5:53 p.m., nine minutes after receiving the call, she pulled into the small court and parked her cruiser in the driveway of the house. She got out of the car, walked up to two women standing there.

"Which one of you called?" Stewart asked.

"I did," said a woman with long blond hair.

The woman seemed quite nervous. Both of them did. They stood close together as they spoke. Stewart looked past them at the house. The glass from the front storm door was broken and shards lay on the porch. She moved closer. At the side of the house sat a box, a box big enough to hold a small microwave oven perhaps. On top of it sat a full green garbage bag. The MDT call had mentioned the bag. The woman who called police said she was afraid to open it, afraid that what she had been told might actually be true. Stewart slipped on a pair of latex gloves as the three of them walked to the side of the house.

"We feel like idiots," said the blond woman.

"Why?" Stewart asked.

"Here's a couple of girls afraid to look in the bag, and then they send a female officer."

"Well, I don't want to look either, but I have to; it's my job. Let's take a look."

Gary Yokoyama

Constable Kathy Stewart, first on the scene.

Stewart grabbed the top of the tied garbage bag and lifted it off the box. The bag had weight to it, maybe eight pounds. She set it down, untied the top knot, looked inside.

There were a few plastic containers inside, like those for margarine. An empty Coke bottle. She looked deeper into the garbage bag. There was an empty white plastic tub. Sitting in the tub was a small bag, a bag that soil or peat moss would come in. She took the bag out.

A sobering thought was running through her brain: if this is a crime scene and I mess it up, Abi-Rashed will kill me. She had just finished one of his training sessions on crime scene management. Detective Sergeant Peter Abi-Rashed, Major Crime Unit. In class he showed photos to illustrate examples of crime scenes where officers had inadvertently, but sloppily, trampled over evidence. The defense lawyers would have a field day with such mistakes in court, was the lesson.

"Now *this* is the *worst* crime scene!" he bellowed to the trainees. He didn't name names, but you never wanted to be the one he's holding up as an example of how not to do things, even anonymously. Word will get around, you'll be found out. Abi-Rashed struck fear in the hearts of new recruits. He came across old-school cop, the booming voice, meticulous work habits, everything by the book. Do not screw up, he'd tell them. We cannot afford to screw up. Screw up and I will find you.

Kathy Stewart reflected that she had made one rookie mistake already at the call on Burns Place. She had parked the cruiser in the driveway. Always park down the road a bit. But this was a tight cul-de-sac, not much room to park on the street.

As the two women watched, Stewart noticed that inside the soil bag was something wrapped in fabric, like a baby's receiving blanket. She peeled back the layer. There was a plastic-wrapped bundle inside. And inside that was a clear bag. It was in that bag. White on one side, deep red on the other. She knew basic biology from university. Follicles. Flesh. The two women watching held each other tightly now.

"What is it?" asked the blond woman, who was shaking now. "Is it from a cat?"

"No," Stewart replied.

The blond woman started to cry.

"Oh my God," she said.

Constable Kathy Stewart called for backup.

# CHAPTER 2 ~ BAPTISM BY FIRE

"Abi-Rashed." Detective Peter Abi-Rashed took the call at his home on the west Mountain. It was from Central Station downtown—and on a Saturday night. He was off duty. Not a good sign. One of the most senior detectives in the Major Crime Unit, or homicide branch, he only got phoned off the clock when there was a suspected murder. And it often meant the next few days would be what detectives called the marathon phase, working around the clock in the critical early moments of an investigation. Might work 35 hours straight off the mark, depending on the case. It's part of the job. Killers don't honor a schedule. But still, he mused, this was the long Easter weekend. Family time. Get some yard work done. He was not pleased.

About to plunge, again, into the dirty work of murder, rejoining his Major Crime Unit colleagues, "the merchants of misery" as he dubbed them, Peter Abi-Rashed showered, shaved, and put on a suit. He was one of the original four detectives when the unit was created in 1992 to focus on Hamilton homicide cases. Abi-Rashed hung a print in his office, a sketch of the original four: Abi-Rashed, Frank Harild, Steve Hrab, and Fred Mueller. From the start, Major Crime had an aura within the Hamilton Police Service. Part of it was the look: on the job its detectives almost always wore a suit and tie. When they showed up at a scene, some of the uniform officers would say, "The big guns are here; the suits are here, the swinging dicks."

As Abi-Rashed became one of the senior men, he insisted on the dress protocol. None of this new talk about going "business casual." In Major Crime you deal in life and death, with victims' families, and the suspects. Wear a suit. Carries authority, seriousness. You are a professional, so dress like it. Casual? The very notion offended him.

Abi-Rashed walked from his house.

"See ya in a couple of days," he cracked to his wife.

Peter Abi-Rashed cut a complex figure. He was built like a retired football running back. Stocky, broad shoulders, thick hands. Befitting his look, he could come across blustery, no time for small talk, cut to the chase, used loud and salty language. He even wrote his e-mails in large type as though trying to convey volume in print. He could also be sensitive and thoughtful. Did lots of community charity work. He seemed rough around the edges, yet also meticulous, a neat freak, a military-style sense of order. In the kitchen at home, all the canned goods were ordered smallest to largest, all of the labels facing the front. In his office, shift so much as a paper clip to a spot it didn't belong and he caught the transgression.

That Saturday night he drove along Fennell Avenue West, left onto Upper James and down the Mountain to the lower city. The call had filled him in on basic details. Suspicious circumstances at a house at 12 Burns Place. The early report from a uniform in the field was that body parts might have been found on scene.

Gary Yokoyama

*Body parts?* He knew little else, but Abi-Rashed's mind was already going full bore, considering the possibilities. He liked to think of homicide investigation as a puzzle, and at this stage there were barely any pieces at all. Hell, in the end there might not even be a puzzle to solve, it might have nothing to do with a homicide. Body parts, tissue of some description found in the garbage. Well? Think about it, he

Detective-Sergeant Peter Abi-Rashed.

reflected. Easter? Certain cultures at Easter time? Think: sheep, lamb. They buy it at the butcher, put the remains out with the garbage. Abi-Rashed might get to do some of that yard work after all. He certainly wasn't looking for a new case, already had plenty on his plate, been up to his neck with the Frost homicide. Two months earlier, February, an 80-year-old Hamilton man named Clyde Frost was found, his bludgeoned body in a Dodge van in Regent Park in downtown Toronto. Hamilton's first homicide of 1999.

He also had ongoing court preparation for what had become known in the city as the Baby Maliek case. It involved the beating death of a 14-month-old toddler named Maliek two years earlier. Abi-Rashed had reported to the hospital the night the boy Maliek died, having suffered brain damage from a skull fracture and other serious injuries. After that night, the detective could not remove the vision of the little boy from his mind's eye. They were going after both Maliek's mother, Carmelita Willie, and her boyfriend, Carlos Clarke. Both had been charged but there were miles to go shepherding the case through the justice system. During the investigation stage, early on, Abi-Rashed had wasted no time in going for the hot button when he interrogated the boyfriend, face to face, no cuffs or restraints in the interview room at Central Station. Abi-Rashed openly accused Clarke of being a pedophile, knowing that would get him, push him over the edge. Clarke charged the big detective, Abi-Rashed kept his hands down, tightened his jaw and braced for the blow, hoping he'd punch him in the face on videotape. But Clarke stopped just short of it—all Abi-Rashed got was a shot of some nasty breath.

He turned left off Victoria Avenue downtown, continued along King William Street to Central Station. It was just after 7 p.m. He beeped himself up to the second floor and into the Major Crime department. A briefing was held for detectives called in to work the new case. There was a buzz in the room. The word they were getting was that the tissue found in the garbage bag was in fact human remains. A potential homicide.

Peter Abi-Rashed was in charge. He started making calls, barking out assignments to the others. "Is the victim male or female? Is there more than one? Where are the other parts? Need to secure the site, now, media is going to be on this, probably already is. Get the command van up there. Officers need to canvass the neighborhood, interview anyone who might have seen or heard anything. Interview the woman who called it in, what's her story? What does she know? Where is the crime scene—is it in fact that house on Burns Place or elsewhere? Gather any and all information on the owner of 12 Burns Place."

"I want to know everything about the guy who lives there," Abi-Rashed bellowed. "I want to know what he had for breakfast this morning."

\* \* \*

Up the Mountain at Burns Place, Constable Kathy Stewart waited nervously outside the house for backup to arrive. Her first crime scene. Don't blow it. When she had exited her cruiser, talked to the two women, and examined the garbage bag at the house, she had not worn her police uniform cap. Now she went back to the cruiser and put it on. Uniform protocol.

Another cruiser pulled up. Stewart expected a veteran to be sent to a scene where she had confirmed that body parts had been discovered. Instead, out stepped a uniform male colleague who had been on the job maybe a year.

"You?" Stewart said. "This is who they send?"

"What do you have?" he asked.

Stewart told him about the human flesh.

"Want to take a look?"

"No."

"What, are you chicken?" she said, then instantly regretted the remark.

"If you made the call, and you know what you saw, you don't need me to look at it," he said evenly.

The officer told her to get ready for the detectives to show any minute, and get her cruiser out of the driveway. Then he reached over and tucked Stewart's gold chain inside her shirt collar out of view. Protocol. At 7:10 p.m., Ident arrived—the forensic identification services van. Out stepped Hamilton police forensic detectives Ross Wood and Gary Zwicker.

The Ident detectives had been working at Central, Zwicker dusting a stolen auto in the police garage for prints ,when the call came in. It had been a busy time for the section, a couple of homicides on the go early in the year. One was a stabbing case, a lot of blood at the scene. Ross Wood had been a cop coming up on 30 years, the last nine in forensic identification. Woody had been Zwicker's training officer, had seen it all, had attended about 50 autopsies during his career and processed crime scenes where the sights and smells of murder were so ripe they sent even hardened cops for counseling. Gary Zwicker, while an experienced officer, was a rookie with the Ident department. He would reflect later that this new case would be a baptism by fire.

"You ready, Zwick?" Wood said. "We got another one."

"Isn't it someone else's turn?" Zwicker cracked.

At the scene, Kathy Stewart escorted Wood and Zwicker up the driveway, showed them the garbage bag, the box, explained what she had done. Ross Wood examined the inside of the bag.

"Yep," he said flatly. "It's skin."

Later, he examined more contents of the garbage bag.

Among the items was a suede jacket wrapped with a foam pad. He cut the tape around the box that Stewart had not opened. Inside, he found more pieces of tissue packed inside bags and small containers. More red flesh. Hair attached to a piece of scalp. Dark reddish hair color, he noted. He noted what appeared to be sections from internal organs.

A thunderstorm was brewing, the air thick with moisture. They needed to get the evidence covered with a tarp and get the body parts to the Hamilton General Hospital morgue for examination.

Kathy Stewart was told she was being relieved at the scene, as she was required down at Central Station to tell her story. She took a breather in her cruiser parked in the street. It was now 9 p.m. and she was starving. She finally opened the bag of Doritos and shoved some chips into her mouth. Tap-tap. Knuckles on the window. Stewart, mouth full, looked up. Abi-Rashed.

"Mmm-yes?" she said, garbling the word.

"They asked me to check on you to see if you're all right," he said. "If you're eating, I think you're all right. Get down to Central and I'll talk to you later."

Good, she thought, she was not in trouble for the munchies. She ate the rest of the Doritos on the drive downtown. Stewart didn't get home until late; she lived about an hour south of the city, near the shores of Lake Erie. It was about 3 a.m., she was still wired. Her husband was asleep on the couch. She woke him, but, going by the book, she couldn't tell him much, just the basics. A difficult thing for a rookie cop to experience, seeing human tissue like that. Wasn't it? Cops were taught about scene shock in training; sometimes it can last a few minutes, sometimes days, or longer. Her excitement for the case, and strong stomach, surprised her.

"Do you think it's weird this isn't bugging me?" she asked him.

Gary Yokoyama

Constable Kathy Stewart.

Her training had kicked in, and she had performed well at an unusual scene, senior officers agreed. She'd had a taste of a murder investigation—and liked it. She decided that night that her goal would be to become a homicide detective. Kathy Stewart went to bed, barely slept, and reported back to work four hours later.

\* \* \*

Media had descended on 12 Burns Place that night, reporters kept at bay by yellow crime scene tape around the property. The coroner on duty, Dr. Richard Porter, arrived. Police still needed a search warrant to do the full exploration of the house, but a decision was made that investigators should take a quick look inside. Human body parts had been left in the garbage outside the house; if the house was in fact the crime scene, there could be another victim inside, and here they were standing around while someone might need help inside. Under the Ontario Coroner's Act, they could lawfully do a walk-through.

Detectives Ross Wood and Gary Zwicker, along with Dr. Porter, approached the front door. They slowly entered the house, careful not to touch anything. Through the living room, bedrooms, bathroom. In the kitchen, smashed dishes, broken furniture. They went upstairs, then back down, descended eight stairs to the basement, around a corner, saw a rec room. Dark red carpet with a black swirl design in it. Pool table dominating the room. Padded brown bar. Mirror paneling on the walls and half-panel wainscoting. Couple of pool cues on the floor. A small fruit cellar, a fan on the floor, more mirror paneling on one wall.

Without a warrant, there was no opportunity to search for clues, to use alternative light sources, spray chemicals that could reveal hidden signs of life and death. But before they exited, Ross Wood's naked eye zoomed in on possible clues as they moved throughout the house: a dark smear on the bathtub and on the frame of the rear door to the house. Blood? Curious thing about the basement, too. Parts of the rest of the house looked like a tornado passed through, he thought, the broken furniture, dishes. But the basement was tidy, for the most part. Smelled clean, too, like disinfectant. His eye picked up on something else. There seemed to be a significant number of flies in the house. And the largest concentration was in the basement.

*The Hamilton Spectator*

Police gather at 12 Burns Place.

# CHAPTER 3 ~ REMAINS

*Saturday night*
*April 3, 1999*

Downtown on Barton Street, vice and drugs was investigating a shooting. Hamilton Police Detective Ken Weatherill was among those on the scene combing the Santa Rosa bar for shell casings. He got a call to leave and report to Central Station. Must be something big to be pulled off the scene, he figured. Weatherill, 36, could pass for Kevin Costner at a glance, and was on the road to becoming an inspector one day with the service. He had a sharp mind and memory. Remembered the date of his first day on the job and every detail of his first call, on October 14, 1986: night shift, uniform patrol, intoxicated person downtown on Mary Street. Later, he served on the tactical emergency team.

Back at the Major Crime Unit, Weatherill was briefed by Peter Abi-Rashed. Body parts found in a garbage bag and box outside of 12 Burns Place. They had to get inside that house, needed a warrant for the place, and fast. A search warrant application provides a running narrative of a working investigation, offering an argument to a justice of the peace why police need to conduct a search. The vice and drugs guys do warrants all the time—searching buildings is what they do. Weatherill was considered a pro at it and was parachuted in to the investigation specifically for that purpose.

"Kenny, we need the warrant," Abi-Rashed said. "Get the warrant."

Weatherill read through Constable Kathy Stewart's notebook, reviewed interview notes she had taken from her conversation with the women outside 12 Burns Place. He was keenly aware that getting a warrant in the early hours of an investigation is crucial. And if you write so much as one misplaced word, a JP could reject it. Or, later, a defense lawyer might jump all over it when the case goes to court. They always go after the warrants, he reflected. He sat down at a computer and typed into the morning.

Meanwhile, forensic pathologist Dr. Chitra Rao approached the steel table in the basement of Hamilton General Hospital. Rao was an expert in the science of murder and she had worked some of Hamilton's highest-profile homicides over the years, among them the murder of Ranjit Khela at the hands of serial poisoner Sukhwinder Dhillon. As always, her mission was to document physical characteristics of the victim, any possible pathology, and ultimately determine the most likely cause of death.

She unwrapped the packages found in the garbage that had been brought to the morgue by the forensic detectives. She spread out the recovered parts, the deep red tissue of organs, muscle, viscera. What had happened? She well knew it was not uncommon for a killer to try and cover tracks after murdering. Doing so is called a "defensive action" by criminal profilers. But there is one kind of defensive action that belongs in an unusual category. It is the rare killer who has it in their soul to cross a Rubicon into the coldest and bloodiest of places; to methodically and clinically cut a victim into pieces to conceal what he has done.

Chitra Rao was up against it trying to tell anything about the victim from the limited remains in front of her. Gender was a mystery, it was even inconclusive if the victim was an adult or a youth. Shelley Saunders, a renowned forensic anthropologist at McMaster University, was contacted. But the parts of a body that Saunders would study to identify age or gender—bones—were not present from the soft tissue on her table.

In an autopsy a forensic pathologist always checks the liver and the heart, to see if death came from natural causes—

from alcohol-induced liver disease, for example—while also checking for signs of trauma to the organs. In this case, the organs available were too limited and suggested no cause of death. As for identity, there were no fingers for rolling prints. It was as though the killer had chosen to extract and separate internal tissues in order to throw off investigators. DNA testing could at least prove gender, but that would take time. Samples were packaged for submission to the Centre of Forensic Sciences in Toronto.

Peter Abi-Rashed heard the update from the morgue. He was well aware that, if in the end all the detectives had to go on to establish identity and cause of death was a DNA test from bits of tissue, the investigation was in deep trouble. But he tried to stay positive, knew it was still early in the game. He was counting on finding the rest of the victim and identifying a crime scene. Detectives title their white homicide casebooks with the surname of the victim. Later he wrote the title of the new case in black ink on the cover. He'd have to keep it gender neutral, for now: "J. Doe."

* * *

Up at 12 Burns Place, Abi-Rashed's cell phone rang. It was an officer at the Major Crime Unit with information regarding a person of interest identified in the case. The person's name was Sam Pirrera. He was 32 years old, the owner and resident of the house. Criminal record data racing across a computer screen from the Canadian Police Information Centre (CPIC) said: *Pirrera, Samuel Joseph. Theft. Drugs. Assault. Marks: pig-ura* (Tattoo of a pig—upper right arm).

Pirrera. The name rang a bell with Abi-Rashed. Took him back to his years before Major Crime, the 1980s, before the suit and tie—old clothes, working the streets downtown, the north end. He remembered. Little Sam Pirrera. That Sam.

So, he thought, have you graduated to the big leagues now, Sam? Abi-Rashed decided he needed to have a face-to-face talk with him downtown.

* * *

*Summer 1984*
*Barton Street, Hamilton*

Smack-smack-smack-smack-smack. Running shoes slapping pavement, a gang of teenagers running along Barton at the sight of an unmarked police car, the game on once again. One of the teenagers was named Sam Pirrera. Small Italian guy. The boys that hung with Sam, maybe a dozen of them, caused trouble, smoked pot, stole from variety stores. They knew they weren't going to do time for it. They taunted the cops.

"I smell bacon!"

"Hey pigs!"

Out of the car jumped a broad-shouldered, 29-year-old plainclothes Hamilton police officer, his standard-issue Smith & Wesson revolver lodged in a shoulder holster under a casual jacket, his dark eyes alive to the chase yet again. His name was Tarek Peter Abi-Rashed. He had been on the job just a few years, was born in Egypt, moved to Canada when he was eight. Dad was a mechanical engineer, Mom a seamstress. He graduated from McMaster University in sociology and geography, but had always wanted to be a cop. Why? "Just wanted to kick ass," he joked. In fact, policing seemed an honorable occupation, an honorable career. It might sound hokey, he reflected, but it was about doing the right thing, taking care of the people who needed it most. You hear people wonder why "they" didn't do something to help. Well, he would be the person who did something.

In the early 1980s he worked the "special squad," a shift that young cops relished. Many of those who worked it went on to high-profile careers as homicide detectives with the service, guys like Warren Korol, Mike Thomas, and Abi-Rashed. You dressed-down, drove around rough parts of town looking for trouble, made arrests. Total freedom of movement. Hit the dark spots, alleyways, bush parties, strip clubs, fly the flag and keep in touch with contacts on the street. It meant long, late hours and lots of time in court following up on charges. No shortage of action. Abi-Rashed was partnered in an unmarked car back then with Al Jones.

"Hey Starsky! Hutch! Pigs!"

Abi-Rashed and Jones sprinted down the street after Sam Pirrera and his gang. Sam was a little guy, only about five-foot-seven on his tiptoes, although he had an outsized defiant attitude like the rest of the troublemakers. There was a relatively harmless ethos to the cat-and-mouse game. It was kind of catch me if you can, Abi-Rashed thought. It was different back then in the early eighties; it was big news if you arrested someone carrying a knife. Back then you could approach a vehicle to make an arrest knowing that you could end up in a fight, but it would be fist to fist, maybe a bat involved. Teenage gangs didn't beat people to death without a second thought, didn't carry firearms, machetes. For the most part, the only weapons wielded by Sam and his crew were their feet and their attitude. Sometimes a charge, sometimes just a warning or a scolding.

Smack-smack-smack-smack-smack. Peter Abi-Rashed and Al Jones closing ground on the gang, a big meaty hand grabbing Sam by the shoulder.

"I'm watching you," Abi-Rashed would warn. "Don't mess up again. Because I will find you."

From special squad, Abi-Rashed moved into the vice and drugs branch, which meant taking down bigger players on the street. All cops in vice and drugs had nicknames, mostly as a practical matter, for communicating with each other on the street. The names were often funny takes on an aspect of their look or personality—one of the guys smoked menthol cigarets and so he got tagged with "Menthol," which was an old-school cop dig at his preference for smokes that were considered marginally healthier than regulars. Abi-Rashed routinely got "Abi," but that wouldn't do for his street name.

Working downtown, cops in vice and drugs didn't wear jackets and ties. They tended to wear trendy stuff. This being the mid-1980s, the decade of *Miami Vice*, Abi-Rashed took to wearing pastel-colored T-shirts, maybe a casual jacket, and on occasion a red Hawaiian-style shirt. One day, while working a surveillance on Vine Street, his partner, John Peatfield, hit on a nickname.

"I know—you're always wearing that Hawaiian shirt. I've got your name. 'Miami.' "

"*Miami*?" Abi-Rashed replied, his thick dark eyebrows arching in contempt. "It's a *Hawaiian* shirt."

"Yeah, a *Miami Vice* shirt. You're Miami."

Back at the station, Peatfield passed along his partner's new nickname and it caught on instantly, was logged in the vice and drugs code name book. And then another cop piped up to Peatfield.

"Well I've got your name then: 'Beach.' 'Miami'. 'Beach.' You're 'Beach.' " After a couple of years, Abi-Rashed moved out of vice and drugs, but Peatfield stayed put, stuck with having to explain to newer officers how it was he got tagged "Beach." It was at that point in a rapidly blooming career that Abi-Rashed got a new post as a detective in CID, criminal investigations division. That meant turning in his T-shirts and silk for a jacket and tie, although the wired street cop lived on inside the new clothes.

Even though he was now supposed to be an investigator, Abi-Rashed couldn't help himself; he still ended up chasing bad guys on the street when he sensed trouble, and got in the occasional scrap. Some old-timers in the office razzed him about it, about this crazy young guy who acted like it was the Wild West out there. Abi-Rashed didn't appreciate the jibes, but he couldn't help following his instincts—which led him into his first lead role in a homicide investigation. It happened in 1988, a rare case of a detective actually arresting a suspect minutes after the crime.

Abi-Rashed had been driving back to the station after midnight, when he saw a guy sprinting down the street, chased by a group of people. It turned out the guy had just stabbed and killed a man in the Party Zone Hotel. Abi-Rashed sped after him, roared the wrong way down a one-way street, parked, hopped out of his car, took the suspect down, and cuffed him. The man was convicted for manslaughter. Homicide became Peter Abi-Rashed's game, the stabbing case just the prelude to many more, the first of about 100 Hamilton homicides in which he would play some investigative role. One of them would stick with him more than any other, and that was the one involving little Sam Pirrera.

# CHAPTER 4 ~ A THOUSAND HITS

*March 4, 1967*
*Hamilton*

The dark eyes took their first peek at the world on Saturday, March 4, 1967. Back then, most babies in Hamilton were delivered at St. Joseph's Hospital, certainly when the parents were Catholic. That was the case with the new baby's parents, Antonio and Lina Pirrera. They named their first-born son Samuel Joseph.

The extended Pirrera family was originally from Sicily, the island that sits off the southern coast of Italy. Right after the First World War, scores of Sicilians from a village called Raculmuto emigrated to Canada. It was said that, in fact, nearly the entire village took a ship across the world, entered the St. Lawrence and Lake Ontario, docked in Hamilton Harbour and put down roots right there. They settled in a neighborhood just up the hill from the waterfront and railway yards, on Bay Street North. To this day, signs in that part of old Hamilton commemorate the neighborhood as Corso Raculmuto.

By the time Sam was born, Antonio and Lina Pirrera had moved into a small split-level home on the East Mountain, on Brucedale Avenue. Sam had an older sister, and would eventually have two other siblings. Sam's father was listed as a contractor, and later a carpenter, in the city directory, but would soon get on full time in the steel mills at Dofasco. In 1968, the family

Sam Pirrera's boyhood home.

Gary Yokoyama

moved back to the lower city, a brick home on Cannon Street East, near Wentworth, not far from a small grocery store run by Sam's grandmother.

Hamilton is many cities. The tender-tough cliché is that of "The Hammer," represented by the city's fading north end, where men like Rocky DiPietro and Angelo Mosca once proudly wore the black and gold of the Tiger-Cats pro football team, playing out of old Ivor Wynne Stadium, which loomed like a dark iron giant among the frame houses lining narrow streets, the smell of Big Steel piercing the nostrils. This is the part of town where Sam Pirrera grew up. That end of Cannon had a heavy Italian flavor to it with surnames like Avarello, DeLorenzis, Gugliemo, Di Liberto—which was Lina Pirrera's maiden name—De Luca, Di Mascio, Perri, Bernardo.

As a young boy Sam attended St. Brigid's school nearby. He would one day tell others that his childhood was happy, but that, when he was nine, his parents were fighting a lot and his father left the home for a time. It left Sam feeling angry; his relationship with his dad was stormy. He forged a close relationship with his grandfather—but he died on June 5, 1979, when Sam was 12.

Sam was a small teenage boy with dark unruly hair when he attended Scott Park Secondary School. His bedroom was

Garv Yokoyama

at the front of the house, in a finished attic, facing Cannon Street. In summertime he cranked the stereo, blasting the noise out the window, trying to outdo his friends doing the same in their own homes. He got a ticket from the police once for "unnecessary noise."

Teenage Sam Pirrera's yearbook photo.

On June 6, 1983, he obtained his driver's licence at 16. Four months later, Sam was charged and convicted for theft under $200 and received 12 months' probation.

In the spring of 1985 he was charged with doing 73 km/ hr in a 50 km/hr zone. Then another speeding ticket, doing 120 km/hr in a 100 km/hr zone in St. Catharines. Another one for driving the wrong way down a one-way street. Another for failing to produce vehicle insurance for an officer.

To cops who worked the streets in the north end, little Sam Pirrera was well known as one of the troublemakers running in relatively harmless gangs. But worse than his tendency toward reckless driving and hell-raising was his experimentation with drugs. First it was pot, but then Sam tried crack cocaine and it changed his life. In the 1980s crack had become available and affordable, giving rise to a crack epidemic in American inner cities, and easy access to the drug in border cities like Hamilton, which is 45 minutes west of the border at Buffalo, N.Y. In March 1985, one week after his eighteenth birthday, Sam was convicted for possession and trafficking in narcotics. In July of that year, he failed to appear for a court date. His relationship with his father had often been rough, but now neither of his parents could tolerate his behavior. They kicked him out of the house for a time; he was a bad influence on the younger members of the family, they said. Sam was eventually invited back, but his problems were just beginning.

There is a saying among crack addicts: a thousand hits are not enough, and one is too much. Sam Pirrera had entered a game he could neither quit nor win. Others would end up paying a high price for the toxic mix of his addiction and the dark peculiarities that colored his soul.

\* \* \*

*Saturday, April 3, 1999*
*8:35 p.m.*
*12 Burns Place*

A crowd had gathered outside the yellow police tape at Sam Pirrera's house, neighbors wondering what was going on, reporters holding their place all night waiting for the latest word from the police. Detective Peter Abi-Rashed stood inside the tape. He knew that what he dubbed "the media horde" was inevitable. He maintained decent relations with journalists, but had no time for those who got in the way, much less those who took his comments out of context. Don't burn me, he would warn, or I will never talk to you again. Ever.

He reflected that the scene wasn't as chaotic as it could have been. Sometimes you get the media buzzing around, breaking news of a homicide on TV before the police have notified anybody. Then you get family members in a panic, racing to the scene to find out what's going on, nearly running over police officers.

His cell rang again.

"Abi-Rashed."

It was a uniform officer calling from St. Joseph's Hospital, which sat directly at the base of Hamilton Mountain. The uniform briefed Abi on the latest information. The person of interest in the case, Sam Pirrera, had in fact checked into the hospital that afternoon. And now there was a situation.

"Jesus," muttered Abi-Rashed.

In St. Joe's, the place where he had been born, Sam Pirrera tried to hang himself with a blanket. He almost succeeded. Someone in the hospital found him just in time and cut him down.

Abi-Rashed called Major Crime detective Wayne Bennett, who had been conducting interviews for the case at the Mountain station. He was Abi-Rashed's lead investigator on the ground.

"Bennett."

"Benny. You are required to attend down at St. Joe's. If Pirrera makes any attempt to leave the hospital, arrest him on reasonable and probable grounds of murder."

Wayne Bennett's pale blue eyes glowed with intensity against his leathery face, and he spoke with a raspy voice that betrayed battles with some of Steeltown's nastier characters during his 30 years on the force. He had worked undercover. A chameleon, he grew his hair past his shoulders, blending into the scenery of Hamilton's underworld, working among outlaw biker gangs. He once posed as a contract killer in order to get a bead on a local thug who was paying for hits; he was hired for a hit and an arrest was made.

But he was taciturn about his experiences, meeting questions about his past with a bottomless stare. "If you feel like you're pulling nails out of a hardwood floor," he told a journalist with a grin, "you are." He would only allow that, over the years, he had dealt with some people "who had a whole lot of different thoughts on life."

On that Saturday of Easter weekend, he had been outside on the back deck at home (where in the city that might be, he would not say). The barbecue had reached the precise temperature, he had seasoned the steak perfectly and was just about ready to sear it on the grill, when he got paged at 6:45 p.m. about a suspicious death case. He showered, shaved, put on a suit, and reported to work. The beef never did hit the coals, he reflected ruefully.

After receiving Abi-Rashed's call, Bennett sped to the hospital, arriving at 8:50 p.m. He learned that Sam Pirrera had been checked in as a "person in distress" and placed in an observation room near the ER, and that he had tried to hang himself with a blanket. At 9:10 p.m., Bennett received a page. It was Abi-Rashed. In those days Bennett didn't carry a cell; he picked up a hospital phone off a counter and dialed.

Hamilton General Hosptial's ER.

Abi-Rashed now said that Pirrera should formally be placed under arrest for murder. The body parts had been found in Pirrera's garbage, and they had been conducting interviews. They had enough information to lay a charge. In the hospital, Bennett spoke to a veteran uniformed officer named Dave Petz and relayed the information. Along with his partner, rookie Jack Vander Pol, Petz entered the observation room in the ER where Sam was kept. Vander Pol stood seven feet tall, and a good thing, too, because the suspect was not going quietly.

Petz read Sam his Charter rights and moved to cuff him. That's when it hit the fan. Sam tried to get away and fight the arrest. Petz and Vander Pol struggled to pin him down. Sam was bare-chested, drenched in sweat, and slippery as a fish. The brawl was on. The suspect was not a big guy, Petz reflected, but adrenalin and perhaps drugs still in his system gave Sam remarkable strength. A few other uniforms jumped in. It occurred to Petz that this was an instance where, if it was one-on-one, he'd probably have to severely injure or even kill the man to get him down and ensure his own safety. But with big Jack Vander Pol and the others, they were able to restrain and cuff him.

Sam continued to grunt and struggle as the officers led him out of the ER. As they approached the sliding ER door, Sam jumped up and braced his bare feet against the glass, pushing with all his might, the pane bowing as though it would break. They peeled him off the glass, and finally he was loaded into the police van for transport to Central Station downtown. Before the van had completed the short drive to Central, the banging started. It was Sam slamming his head and face against the inside wall of the wagon, drawing blood. They had to turn around and head back to St. Joe's.

When anyone in police custody has any type of injury in transport, no matter how minor it is, Hamilton police protocol is to have the suspect treated and medically cleared before incarceration downtown. It's not uncommon for someone to bang his head against the wall of the van, acting out, often when drunk or high. That's why the interior wall is made of acrylic plastic. Was Sam trying to kill himself again? It would be nearly impossible to commit suicide that way; he'd go unconscious before he could kill himself banging his own head on something like Plexiglas.

Returned back to the ER, wheeled in on a stretcher, he started to moan, and thrash against the restraint straps holding him down. He was taken for an X-ray but refused to cooperate, struggled to get off the stretcher, so the X-ray was not done. He was treated for a laceration over his right eye; a nurse cleansed the cut. She noted other abrasions and bruising on his head. His transport to Central Station lockup would have to wait until the next morning.

Meanwhile, at 9:20 p.m., Detective Wayne Bennett introduced himself to Sam's mother, Lina Pirrera, who was also at the hospital. He escorted her to the quiet room for an interview. From interviews conducted so far, police knew that Lina Pirrera had been inside his house on Burns Place earlier that day. Bennett wanted to get any details of Sam's recent actions that she knew about. She sounded very upset. She said Sam had called her that day seeking help. He didn't sound good, like he needed medical attention for his mental state. She went over to see him at his house. Lina Pirrera said that Sam had substance abuse problems in the past. Was he abusing at the present time? She told Bennett she wasn't aware of that.

Bennett spoke to her for 40 minutes. Just before 10 p.m., he finished the interview. He spoke to the ER charge nurse, made sure that Mrs. Pirrera was offered counseling by St. Joe's staff. But she declined assistance and instead left the hospital. Bennett headed to Central Station. Just after midnight, a few members of Sam's family met him on the second floor in the lobby of the Major Crime unit—his two sisters, a brother, and a girlfriend of the brother.

"Sam has been arrested for first-degree murder and is under treatment at St. Joseph's Hospital," Bennett told them. He added that injuries Sam had sustained were self-inflicted. His family reacted with disbelief and burst out crying. Bennett contacted police victim services for them. Then he briefed Abi-Rashed and returned to his home at 5 a.m. Sunday to catch a few hours' sleep before resuming the marathon.

At 5:30 a.m. Sunday morning, vice and drugs detective Ken Weatherill finished writing the final lines of a 13-page search warrant for the house: "The informant verily believes that contained on the property and inside the residence at 12 Burns Place is evidence that is necessary to substantiate the charge of 1st Degree Murder and prays a warrant be issued," he wrote.

He faxed his completed warrant application to a justice of the peace on duty at the 24-hour telewarrant center near

Police stand guard at 12 Burns Place.

Toronto. At 7:13 a.m. the response came through on the fax machine. Weatherill handed a signed warrant for the house to Abi-Rashed, who immediately made a phone call to officers up at the scene at 12 Burns Place.

"We are now acting under authority of a Criminal Code warrant," he said.

# CHAPTER 5 ~ ILL AND MENACING

Up at the house, Ident had started searching outside for clues. Forensic detectives Ross Wood and Gary Zwicker were joined by fellow Ident man Curt Napholc, who had been seconded from working a murder, a stabbing, at a home on the Beach Strip along Hamilton's lake front. Napholc was of Hungarian descent and his name was one that his colleagues could neither spell nor pronounce. A rough pronunciation sounded similar to Naples, so when he was a cadet, 15 years earlier, he got "Napes" as a nickname. There was heavy physical work required to turn over the property in this new case, and Napes, a muscular six-foot-two and 250 pounds, fit the bill.

Apart from the body tissue, they had nothing else, did not have a crime scene, no hard evidence that a murder, or any other crime, had actually taken place at that address. In theory, someone could have dumped the body parts by Sam's house. Ident had to find the rest of them, and evidence of a homicide. They looked around the property, the side of the house, the back yard, to see if there was any sign of fresh digging where parts might be buried. Seeing none, they kept looking. If the killer was smart, he wouldn't leave signs of burial. He would conceal it.

Cops make fun of TV dramas where the crime scene investigators do everything—interview the accused, make arrests, shoot the bad guys. But when it comes to turning over a potential crime scene, CSIs do in fact do it all. Out came the shovels, with younger officers Zwicker and Napholc doing most of the grunt work as Ross Wood, the veteran, made notes and supervised. They removed gravel from inside a shed in the back, right down to the dirt, took apart a homemade wooden porch by the pool. No sign of anything.

Wood got a page. There was another possible lead and it would mean an even dirtier job for them. Detective Wayne

Bennett had looked into the garbage angle: if parts were left out in the garbage, might the rest of the victim already have been put out with an earlier round of garbage? Bennett contacted the city's public works department to determine when the trash had last been collected on Burns Place and where it went. The bad news was that the garbage had been collected a few days earlier and already incinerated and taken to landfill, the ashes mixed with other piles. Even if they could find bones in the ashes, they had lost continuity of the trash. The good news was that public works pinpointed the compactor truck that had done the collection outside Sam Pirrera's house a few days earlier. The truck was now empty, but there might still be trace evidence of human remains linked to those found at the house.

As the new guy with Ident, Gary Zwicker knew who would get tagged with the assignment. Next thing he knew, he was crawling around inside city garbage truck No. 47. He wore a protective suit and a mask. But it still stunk. Horrible. He was in there for a few hours, trying alternative light, white light, spraying luminol, a chemical that, when it comes in contact with blood, will glow blue. The test came up positive. There was blood in the truck. But what did that prove? It could be animal blood, could be from hamburger meat. They collected samples for submission to CFS in Toronto.

Gary Yokoyama

Forensic Detective Gary Zwicker.

* * *

Rap. Rap. Rap.

Detective Wayne Bennett knocked his knuckles against the glass wall of the lockup cell in the basement of Central Station. It was just after 10 a.m. Sunday. Sam Pirrera lay on his back on the bed, having been transferred to the station from hospital. He wore the white jumpsuit issued by Hamilton police to all those in custody, made of paper-like disposable material. His other clothing had been seized as evidence, even the boxer shorts he had been wearing with the Corona beer motif on them.

Sam looked terrible, but then Bennett had seen his share of men after a night in lockup. They never look their best. This guy was no exception. He lay there, saying nothing.

Rap. Rap. Rap.

"No response," Bennett wrote in his notebook. He checked out a car from the carpool and headed back up the Mountain to 12 Burns Place, helped officers who continued to canvass neighbors in the area. After 11 a.m., Peter Abi-Rashed called Benny again; "Sam is awake," he said, "come on back to the station." Down in lockup, at 11:30 a.m., the two detectives looked through the glass at Sam Pirrera, who was still lying down, his eyes closed.

The cell has a glass wall so those in custody don't have bars available to try to hang themselves on. You can talk through the glass if you raise your voice a bit.

"Sam!" boomed Abi-Rashed's deep voice. "Been a long time. What the hell's going on?"

Sam stirred but did not sit up.

"You know why you're here?"

"No," he finally murmured.

"It's a first-degree murder charge."

"What?"

"You were arrested and charged with first-degree murder."

Detectives Wayne Bennett (front) and Peter Abi-Rashed.

"Don't know what you're talking about," he said, his speech slurred.

The early hours of an investigation offer the best time for detectives to conduct an interview, before the suspect is lawyered up. But Sam Pirrera was clearly in no condition to offer a coherent interview. He was still under the influence of whatever treatment he had received at the hospital, or, more likely, whatever substance he had been bingeing on lately. They decided to wait before trying again.

\* \* \*

Later that day, Sunday at 4:30 p.m., Abi-Rashed took another crack at Sam. He was escorted from the lockup cell and taken up an elevator from the basement at Central Station, let off at the second floor near the Major Crime Unit, through another door, down a hallway, a right turn past a thick steel door into a small interview room. Sam Pirrera sported a black eye, the result of having pounded his forehead against the inside wall of the police van. His dark unruly hair looked greasy, his skin pale. He looked ill and menacing at the same time.

Inside the room were a desk and two padded chairs; one of the chairs was chained to the floor so an accused can't hit an officer with it. Sam sat there, with Abi-Rashed in the other chair, which was on wheels.

"Do you know where you are right now Sam?" Abi-Rashed asked.

"Yes," he replied.

"Where?"

"Cop shop."

"Speak up, Sam. We want to get it on tape, so no one can say you didn't say something."

Sam was not cuffed for the interview. Abi-Rashed knew it's best when conducting an interview to allow the suspect some freedom of movement. But at the same time, you want to get as close to the accused as possible. Get in his space. Not that it's always a pleasant experience taking in the odor of a guy who has been in lockup overnight. And he might attack you on top of it. When Abi worked with Al Jones on the special squad, a suspect in custody punched Jones in the face, and Abi, watching on a monitor next door, burst in the room and jumped the guy. Jones was left with a broken jaw.

Gary Yokoyama

Detective Peter Abi-Rashed in the interrogation room.

"OK," Abi-Rashed said to Sam. "Today's date is April 4, 1999, the time is 4:50 p.m. You are in the Hamilton police headquarters. Do you know who I am?"

"Yes. Peter Abi-Rashed."

"You remember me?"

"I think so."

He was surprised that Sam remembered him from the old days.

"OK. Listen up, Sam. You're under arrest for first-degree murder."

Abi-Rashed picked up the caution card that police officers use when arresting a suspect. He read Sam Pirrera his rights; he did not have to talk to police, he had the right to call a lawyer, anything he did say to police could be used in the investigation.

"How do you feel?" Abi-Rashed asked.

"Not good," Sam replied.

"In which way not good?"

"My mindset."

"In what way your mindset?"

"Spiritually. Everything."

"Nervous?"

"Yeah. And spiritually. Inside emotions. And my mind's all f----d up right now."

Abi-Rashed left the room and returned with a glass of water for Sam, then offered him an opportunity to step outside the room and call a lawyer. He escorted him to a phone. Sam made a call to a Hamilton criminal lawyer named James Vincelli. He couldn't reach him. They re-entered the room and sat back down.

"OK, we're back in," said Abi-Rashed. "What do you want to do? You are willing to waive a lawyer right now and talk to me anyway? You can stop and talk to your lawyer if you want. This is what we talked about?"

"Yes."

"So right now you are waiving your rights to talk to a lawyer?"

Sam nodded silently.

"Is that yes?"

"Yes."

Abi-Rashed continued.

"What were you doing yesterday, Saturday?"

"I was freebasing a lot of cocaine."

"What were you doing Friday?"

"Same thing."

"Freebasing coke?"

"All week."

"When did you start?"

" Monday night."

"Why did you start?"

"I was lonely; I was depressed."

"You just go get the coke and freebase? Do you work?"

"Yeah."

"Where?"

"Dofasco."

"Where?"

"Metal tool. We pour steel."

"Were you working last week?"

"I was on stress leave."

"You talk to anyone during the week? Go anywhere? Anyone visit you to see if you're OK?"

"Yeah, my parents."

"What day was that?"

"Wednesday maybe."

"What did you do Thursday?"

"More or less the same thing. Just sit in my basement f-----g freebasing cocaine."

"Do you know how to get help?"

"I know how to go to NA meetings and AA meetings, blah blah blah. Know how to stay clean and sober. I'm just really lonely and that makes me go relapse."

"You are charged with first-degree murder and that stems from an investigation conducted at 12 Burns. Is that your house?"

"Yes."

"Who do you live there with?"

"Right now, or?"

"Let's start with right now."

"Me and my wife and three kids. Until we separated."

Sam Pirrera's estranged wife's name was Danielle.

# Chapter 6 ~ Rock Bottom

*Five years earlier*
*Hamilton, Ontario*

Danielle was a small-town girl from the east coast—Newfoundland—who moved to Hamilton when she was about 20, joining a few family members who had already made the journey to start a new life. In the city she found work as an exotic dancer in the north end, at places like Hanrahan's, which was rough around the edges even by the standards of strip clubs.

A relative of her aunt's had been dating a man, and early in 1994 Danielle was introduced to him. His name was Sam Pirrera. He took notice of her immediately. Young Danielle had blue eyes, long blond hair, was slim and with curves in the right places, just the type that Sam preferred. She also had a big smile and an infectious laugh, came across down to earth, like a country girl—which, basically, she was. She had little education, a couple of grades of high school, but had a way about her: men and women wanted to be around her.

"You remind me a lot of my ex-wife," Sam told Danielle, the first words he ever spoke to her.

Sam was 27, had dark wavy hair and a pronounced forehead, usually a shadow of beard on his face and a mustache. He was short but carried himself with a tough-guy attitude. He almost always wore T-shirts, a jean jacket or an expensive leather jacket. His eyes were very dark, the pupils large. He was the kind of guy a woman might instantly find darkly handsome, or find no redeeming physical trait at all. Danielle was about seven years younger than he was, and Sam managed to sweep her off her feet, wooed her, wined and dined her, and gave her gifts, clothes, the full princess treatment.

"He's a sweetheart, a real gentleman," she told her friends.

At that time, Sam had two young children from his first marriage, a seven-year-old daughter, Ashlee, and a four-year-old son, Matthew. His first wife, a woman named Beverly Davidson, had left him, and the kids, moved out to California to start a new life, he lamented. He was working full-time at Dofasco, in the melt shop of the steelmaker whose stacks belched smoke and flame on Hamilton Harbour, not far from where he grew up in the north end.

He told Danielle that he had once had a drug problem, but had been off the hard stuff, crack cocaine, for several years now. He was turning his life around. But in fact Sam Pirrera never reached accommodation with his life, or with those close to him, for very long. Unpredictable and violent behavior always lurked below the surface, sometimes fueled by drinking, and most of all by his longtime addiction to crack. Not long after he met Danielle, he was laid off from his job at Dofasco. He found some work with National Steel Car for a time. And then, on April 12, 1994, he was convicted for assault, received a suspended sentence and 12 months' probation.

Gary Yokoyama

Sam Pirrera got married a second time.

Still, his relationship with Danielle flourished. In the fall, Sam and Danielle moved into a house on the Mountain, at 12 Burns Place, along with Sam's two kids. It was a small place, one and a half storys, with a sloping roof. It was just a couple of blocks away from the house on Brucedale Avenue where Sam had lived for a time when he was first born.

Danielle continued to work late shifts dancing downtown. And Sam took her on a trip to Las Vegas the following summer, for Fourth of July celebrations in the city that glowed with neon and make-believe. They were married on the big day itself, July 4, 1995. Early in the marriage Danielle began to see disturbing changes in Sam, enflamed by his renewed consumption of liquor and freebasing crack—heating it and inhaling the fumes.

What was it about Sam? Did crack create the monster? Or did the monster exist inside him and the drugs merely accelerate the inevitable? In most relationships Sam was in, he had to be the dominant figure. Women offered him an opportunity to assert control, especially over those who worked in exotic dancing, or prostitution, with the subordination to men the work implied. But then, it was as though his instinctive paranoia, bolstered by crack, led him to sense his dominance being threatened. Crack also helped guarantee a retarded and frustrating sex life. The drug stimulates the pituitary gland, the user feels as though he is experiencing orgasm, without actually having one. It tricks the user into believing he's primed for sex, that he can fly—while, at the same time, most men are

Gary Yokoyama

unable to get an erection when high on crack. And so, if bingeing on crack promised relief from the self-hatred or whatever social pathology dwelled inside Sam, it could also only serve to torture him.

The cycle of the addict is one of extreme highs and debilitating crashes. The user obsessively reaches to recapture the euphoria from the first time, but never achieves it. From then on he lives

Sam's crack cocaine addiction dominated his life.

day to day at a dysfunctional level, underachieving in every facet of his life. Sam feared losing things—his children, his home, cars, women. Try as he might, drugs and drinking did not provide a relief from his insecurities, and the anger that grew from them. How to deal with such rage? Abuse yourself with crack, chase it down with booze on the side, numb yourself, aim for hitting rock bottom and slaying the demons at the same time? Is it enough? Or do you take it out on others, blame them, beat on them, drag them down with you? Because, more than anything, you fear languishing in that black hole alone. Sam could not take the thought of anyone leaving him, certainly not any woman.

His rages became more frequent, he acted out physically, assaulted Danielle.  He was violent towards several women in his life but also, on occasion, towards men he deemed a threat. He told Danielle stories about his past, tales of violence towards other women, conveying a message that was as subtle as a sledgehammer: Don't cross me. He was spinning out of control, brazenly bringing crack-addict prostitutes to the house he shared with his new wife as well as his daughter and son. Danielle had threatened to divorce him.

Despite the unraveling of the relationship, Sam and Danielle had a baby. She gave birth in the summer of 1998 to a girl. Sam had by then been rehired at Dofasco; perhaps there was room for optimism. He proudly carried his baby girl around Burns Place, showing her off to neighbors. But at the same time his addictions and his instinct for destroying himself and those close to him never left. In the last week of June, when Danielle was visiting family with the baby back east in Newfoundland, Sam was at home in the midst of a five-day crack binge. That same week he assaulted his eldest child, daughter Ashlee, who was ten. Among other things, he dragged her up the stairs by her hair and gave her a bloody nose.

Ashlee had been confirmed in her Catholic church about two years before, the pretty little girl with the heart-shaped face wore a long formal white dress for the occasion, her hair long, brown and wavy. She was a spiritual girl who said her prayers every night. But life on Burns Place was rough. Ashlee had been forced to grow up in a hurry, and even more so after Danielle had the baby. Her father and her stepmom were hardly dependable parents, and Ashlee had a nurturing instinct, both for her little brother and, often by necessity, the new baby in the house. She loved her new half sister, but also had to miss school on occasion because someone had to properly look after the baby and she was increasingly the only one able to do it. Sometimes it felt like she was the one raising the child. Other times, Ashlee was too banged up to go to class, she was ashamed to show her bruised face at school. Her attendance at elementary school was terrible.

When they were little, the kids had enjoyed moments with the dad that they loved: outdoor barbecues, riding on his back playing horse. It wasn't all bad. But he was also a wildcard who could become an abusive, raging maniac, fueled by his addictions. Sam set aside a room in the house for himself where he could freely blow his top when he snapped and his anger exploded, a room where he would go on his own to yell and bust up furniture. He told the kids: if they ever hear him yelling or breaking things inside that room, do not come in. No matter what, stay out.

The time that Danielle returned from her trip out east, she saw that the house was a disaster inside, and that Ashlee had been assaulted. She phoned a social services agency. An official came to the house, spoke to Ashlee, and asked the girl what she wanted to do next. Ashlee said she didn't want to do anything. She didn't want her dad to go away; she loved him. He was crazy, but he was still her dad.

In July, members of Sam's extended family took a day trip to Valens Conservation Area just outside Hamilton. For years it had been a favorite destination for the Pirreras, who enjoyed going to the lake and the beach there. At one point in the afternoon, Sam sat on a rubber inner tube out on the water with Ashlee. He talked to her quietly in private about that week in June.

"I wasn't myself," he said. "I'm so sorry."

Later in July, he was referred by Dofasco to a detox center where he underwent an interview with an official. In a report the official described him as a "tearful, earnest young man, motivated for treatment. He is quiet and cooperative."

"I feel like a piece of shit," Sam told the official. "I want to be a good dad ... keep pushing the kids away; it's the coke ... I've worked hard, have a house, two cars. I don't want to lose them. My wife is beautiful. I love her to pieces."

* * *

In October 1998, Sam flew into another rage and Danielle ran from the house to a neighbor's place with the baby at 2 a.m. That same month, drunk, he got into an argument with Danielle and spat in her face. She called police, he was arrested, charged with assault, and thrown in jail for the weekend. Sam's family hired a lawyer, and his mother, Lina Pirrera, asked Dofasco's medical services department if they would write a letter to the court saying that her son was needed back at work. A Dofasco official told her that was something they did not do.

The next month he was convicted on two more occasions for assault. On the first he received 30 days' intermittent and two years' probation. Sam's mother called Dofasco and told them her son was in jail. After the second assault, Danielle left him, took their baby, and went to live with her mother in Hamilton. Through Dofasco he was signed up for anger-management therapy and also admitted to a substance addiction treatment center called Moreland, where Dofasco sent employees in need. Moreland sat on the Mountain's brow, overlooking the lower city. Sam was assigned a room at the facility and required to stay for at least three weeks, where he was kept cold sober from drugs and alcohol. Upon release from the facility—"graduation" as it was called—he was advised to attend Narcotics Anonymous meetings.

In January 1999, he went to a meeting held in the basement of Grace Anglican Church downtown, not far from where Sam's parents lived. He stood up and took his turn addressing the group.

"I just can't stop using," he said.

Sam averted his eyes from the others, staring at the floor, rarely looking anyone in the face. A guest speaker addressed the group, then took comments from the floor. The speaker, "Dan," had himself been an addict years earlier, had gone at it hard before completing the 12-Step Program to recovery. At the meeting he came off as streetwise, a regular guy who did not beat around the bush. And when an addict stood and mouthed the usual excuses for failing to take control of their life, Dan gave it to them straight. He had once been in their shoes.

"You can't bullshit a bullshitter," he said.

Impressed by his talk, Sam approached Dan after the meeting. While Sam didn't say much at the meetings, to the extent that he talked, he hinted at an addiction and troubled past that none of the others could imagine. Dan had heard that kind of talk before among users who liked to think their experiences were crazier than anyone else's, making their road to recovery steeper as well.

Sam Pirrera was short and unimposing physically. But what instantly struck Dan were his eyes. He had seen variations on that look before in drug abusers, but Sam was different: his eyes were very dark, with large pupils like black marbles. Dan had seen a similar look in guys who were stoned, but Sam's were like that all the time, high or not. Looking into his eyes was like staring into the bottom of a black well, like there was nothing there. Dan found it almost too disturbing to look into them at all.

He agreed to be Sam's sponsor, to attend meetings with him, encourage him to follow the 12-Step Program. Dan did not take on guys who were not willing to help themselves. In Sam's case, a third party had asked him to give Sam a shot, and so he did. Admitting an addiction is step one. Sam had at least gone that far. He told Dan about his crack cocaine use, about picking up hookers for sex and drugs, but he did not offer any other details from his past or personal life, nor mention his kids or Danielle, or his abuse of her.

Dan attended more than a dozen meetings with Sam over the next two months. At the end of most of those meetings, he gave Sam a ride home. They rode in Dan's black pickup truck. He never drove him up the Mountain to Sam's house on Burns Place, though. Sam always asked to be let off near his parents' place on Cannon Street in the north end. They would chat a bit in the truck, but Sam never had much to say, other than claiming that he was working at overcoming his addiction. He was going to regular meetings, but another user who also attended felt that it always looked like Sam was there only because he was forced to be there, that he looked like a prisoner.

On February 24, 1999, he showed up for work at Dofasco looking especially haggard, from drinking and freebasing. Danielle had left him with their daughter and found a place to live downtown. His two kids from his first marriage, Ashlee and Matthew, had started to live full-time at Sam's parents' home. At the end of the month he went on stress leave after telling a Dofasco health counselor that he feared losing his job and that his marriage to Danielle had collapsed. He believed she had been seeing another man, and he was also having "mother-in-law problems."

# CHAPTER 7 ~ CREEPY AURA

One day, Danielle Pirrera walked into a neighborhood bar called Pete's, at Lawrence Road and Cochrane in the north end. Pete's was a place where you went to talk to locals if you were new to that part of town. Danielle had recently moved into a place nearby and was doing some laundry next door. Pete's was a handy pit stop.

A woman named Becky Hunter worked behind the bar. Becky had recently landed the job, had a friendly face and bright smile. She started chatting with Danielle, turned out they had a fair bit in common. Both had marriages that were on the rocks, and they shared the same birthday. Danielle became a semi-regular at Pete's, and friends with Becky.

Becky was among the women who had been through the rabbit hole of violence in Hamilton and had so far lived to tell about it. She was born in nearby Burlington but grew up in Harrisburg, a hamlet near a small town called Paris, west of Hamilton. She went to high school out there, lived with her dad and stepmother, hated it, moved to Hamilton. She fought with her mom, got kicked out of the house a few times, moved out. The small-town girl got sucked into the dangerous underbelly of Steeltown. She started dating a member of the Red Devils biker gang, a guy she met at a bike shop, a smooth talker, she thought. At the same time, she started dating a tattooist everyone knew as Big Dave whose claim to fame was that he had once survived a shooting in which he took seven bullets. Becky hung out at the Red Devils' clubhouse down in Hamilton's Beach Strip community along the Lake Ontario shoreline. Lot of weird stuff going on there. One night she had a bodyguard accompany her to a party at the clubhouse on Arden Avenue, the same house where a Red Devil had been riddled with bullets while leaning against the bar, killed by a sniper perched up on the Queen Elizabeth Way, the expressway that ran past the neighborhood. The Devils reinforced the walls of the place after the murder.

Becky was on the fast track to a life that could possibly end very badly. Over the years she saw and heard too much. A friend of hers, Fran Piccolo, was stabbed to death, along with her two children in a Stoney Creek townhouse. Fran had been through "the life," too, getting messed up with the wrong people. It was as though Becky was both a spectator and participant in a story that could well have been her own. That's what this town can do to you, she thought.

One day, she heard sirens on the street behind where she lived downtown. It was police and ambulance reporting to the scene of the stabbing murder of a boy named Zachary Antidormi, at the hand of his daycare babysitter. All the other kids who were in daycare were taken by police next door to the house of a woman named Karen, one of Becky's best friends. Karen, as it happened, had been close with Sam Pirrera's first wife, Beverly, and Karen used to babysit Sam and Bev's two kids.

When Becky lived downtown in the mid-1990s, a new neighbor moved in, a young woman named Maggie Karer, a pretty girl, but clearly she too was trapped in the life. Becky would sit out on her porch with her husband, and strangers were always dropping by next door. Maggie was hooking, and before long she started to show the tell-tale twitch of crack abuse. Becky resolved not to let it happen to her. If you make the right moves, she thought, you can control your fate.

She kept working at Pete's bar, but started to notice that her new friend Danielle had stopped coming in. Just like that. No call, nothing. What happened to Danielle, she wondered?

* * *

Early in March 1999, Sam Pirrera claimed to a Dofasco health counselor that he had a week of clean and sober living under his belt. He wrote in a self-evaluation form that he had been "feeling lonely, betraded [sic], hurt, sorry for myself, weak, sick of feeling this way." He said he had not relapsed, and had started to return to work, which he said was going better. He noted that he had continued to attend Alcoholics Anonymous and Narcotics Anonymous meetings, had joined the Dofasco gym and was trying to get back in shape. He added that his sister had a baby girl and that his house was "almost clean."

Inside his locker at Dofasco, Sam kept several small newspaper clippings, from the *Toronto Sun*, and a feature the tabloid newspaper ran called Poet's Corner:

> *"For Better or Worse"*
> *If being weak is a part*
> *Of getting stronger*
> *Then I'll stay weak*
> *If crying is part of well being*
> *I'll stop crying*
> *If pain is the way to become alive again*
> *Then I'll stop hurting*
> *If fear is the way to feel joy again*
> *I'll stay fearless*
> *But you know what?*
> *You may be right, I shall fight for it.*

> *"The Other"*
> *Hopes and dreams, nightmares and fears*
> *Can one exist without the other*
> *To love and to honor, to bicker and fight*
> *Can one exist without the other*
> *To grow old together to grow older alone*
> *Can one exist without the other.*

On Friday night, March 26, Sam sat in a circle with others at an Alcoholics Anonymous meeting. Everyone took turns telling their story; Sam spoke about his addictions and recent stresses in his life. His wife had left him, he said, and he was pretty sure she was seeing someone else. It made him angry, but he was trying to pull himself together, trying to stay off the booze and drugs. His wife had also been on drugs, he said, but he wanted to get clean, was working hard at it.

At the same time, as Sam lamented his struggle, he had noticed the blond woman in the circle. She was 38 years old, five-foot-five, had long hair, deeply tanned skin from regular trips to the tanning salon, was slim, curvaceous. Her name was Jean. She had never seen him before. Jean felt the dark eyes on her through the whole meeting. After a while, it made her uneasy and she was thinking, "OK, could you stop that?"

After the meeting she had a smoke and talked to her sponsor in the hallway. She told the sponsor that she didn't own a vehicle, having recently split with her husband, so might have some trouble getting to meetings. The man who had been staring at her hovered nearby, listening. And now he walked over and spoke up.

"Where do you live?" Sam asked.

"East 36th."

"That's really close to where I live. If you ever need a ride, I can help."

They exchanged phone numbers, Sam gave Jean his number from Burns Place, and also his parents' number, because he spent a lot of time there, he said. Dating among participants at AA meetings was discouraged, Jean knew. But she told herself it was just about getting some help for a ride. She had been taken aback by his staring, but when he talked he sounded like a nice enough guy. She was going through a separation with her husband at the time, who had their family car and also owed her a bunch of money. Jean wasn't working at that time, but had once held a factory job at a pulp and paper mill, just as her father had. And, also like her father, she had fallen into alcoholism. For Jean it had started in her mid-30s, drinking anything she could get her hands on. But she grew determined not to follow her dad to the grave via the bottle; he had died young at 67.

After the meeting that night, Jean found her own way home. And about an hour later, just after 10 p.m., her phone rang. It was Sam Pirrera. Did she want to get together tonight, he asked, just hang out, get some pop and chips? She thought about it. She was lonely. And her kids were gone for the weekend, away with their dad. Why not, she thought? Could be fun. Who knows, maybe it could turn into something down the road. She agreed. Sam added that he had a hot tub in his house; she should bring over her bathing suit. Jean didn't tell anyone where she was going.

Sam came over and picked up Jean in his white Cougar, stopped at a variety store for snacks and drinks, then went over to his house. They sat in his kitchen talking for a bit. He told her she looked good. Sam wore jeans and a T-shirt and she thought he was attractive, not as tall as she liked her men, but he had a dark complexion, dark hair, she liked the look. He motioned to the hot tub, which sat in a tiny addition on the back of the house.

"I can get you a T-shirt to wear if that would make you more comfortable," he said.

That was a nice touch, Jean thought, a gentlemanly move. They walked upstairs, he showed her the kids' rooms, one of the beds had a red comforter with a Mickey Mouse design on it. Odd, Jean thought, the house was very clean, like immaculate, not just tidy. For a man's house, she couldn't believe it. And yet, he kept the door to his bedroom closed. While she waited, he slipped into his bedroom with the door open just a crack, closed the door, slipped out again and gave her a shirt.

She changed into her two-piece bathing suit in the bathroom. Back downstairs they eased into the water in the hot tub. Jean still wore the shirt. They talked. A cat was meowing somewhere nearby, repeatedly. Jean couldn't see it. Sam grumbled that it was his wife's cat; it had been meowing like that since she had left him. Didn't sound like he held much affection for the pet. Sam mentioned his first wife, Beverly. She left him years ago, left him and the kids. One year she came back at Christmas time, but he wouldn't let her in the house. She was a bad mother.

He talked about his addictions. The liquor binges led to the coke, he said, when the high from the booze wasn't enough. He told her a story about how he once hid in a crawlspace for a couple of days when his circuits were fried, paranoid, fearing that the police would come looking for him, afraid he had done something, just what, he wasn't sure. When he finally emerged from hiding, he actually went to the police station, he said, to see if they had been looking for him.

"I told them my name, and they said, 'no, we're not looking for you.'"

Jean listened to the story, and started to wonder more about him. It was all sounding pretty weird. He had so far been polite, but she started to get an odd feeling. What if she had made a mistake? She didn't know anything about him. When she had been changing upstairs, what if he had just burst through the door on her? What if he had been watching her somehow?

Sam did not make a move to get closer to Jean in the hot tub, didn't so much as try to hold her hand. Jean had been on dates with guys who tried to make a move, groped at her, wouldn't take no for an answer at first. Sam was doing none of that, and yet her sense of vulnerability grew. It was just the way he looked at her, the downcast eyes, it was kind of creepy, this aura about him. The temperature outside dropped, the room cooled.

"I'm going to freeze when I get out," she said.

"You'll be amazed at how good it feels."

And it did feel good, the temperature in the room seemed perfect after the heat of the water. They sat on lawn chairs in the room, finishing their pop. Then they changed into dry clothes. Sam showed her down to the basement rec room. He seemed very proud of his place. She noticed the fully stocked bar. Bizarre.

"And you're attending meetings?"

"Doesn't bother me," he said.

He asked her to play a game of pool with him.

"No thanks."

Sam persisted. Just one game. She declined again. He did not let up, and her discomfort returned. Why was he being like this? She didn't feel right in the basement. Finally he gave up, they walked upstairs and sat in the living room watching TV. He was stretched out lying at one end of the couch, she was sitting rigidly at the far end meeting his feet. It was after midnight and Jean was upset, even as Sam had not directly said or done anything unusual, apart from his behavior in the basement. She just had a gut feeling, she was freaking out inside. She couldn't focus on what was on the TV. She had never felt like that before, just this sense that she should not make this guy mad.

"I should really get home," she said.

He asked her to stay.

"Come on, don't you get lonely?" he asked.

"I've got four kids, I don't have time to feel lonely," she said.

She waited a few minutes for another opportunity.

"I should get going."

"Can't you just crash here?" he asked, his voice on edge.

She waited again then affected her nicest tone possible.

"I can just call a cab, it's OK."

He started to grow agitated, his voice rising.

"I'm sick of people leaving me."

# CHAPTER 8 ~ "I KILLED SOMEONE"

On Good Friday, April 2, Sam attended a Narcotics Anonymous meeting. It was held in the basement of St. Paul's Presbyterian Church on James Street North, a big gothic building reputed to be haunted by ghosts. As usual Sam wore jeans, a T-shirt, and a high-end, soft Italian leather jacket. He tended to wear the jacket through entire meetings, never taking it off. His NA sponsor, Dan, met him there. After the meeting they walked behind the church to the parking lot and got into Dan's truck.

"How did you think the meeting went?" Dan asked.

"Good. Pretty good."

Dan hadn't known Sam long enough to read him that well. All he knew was that Sam was making little progress in the 12-Step Program. He knew that Sam's employer, Dofasco, had sent him for treatment. Had Sam consented simply to save his job? Or did a part of him genuinely want to get better? Dan thought Sam was somewhere along that road, but not very far. Step 1 is admitting your addiction. Step 2 is believing in what is called a "higher power," something greater than yourself to restore sanity, which leads to Step 3, turning your will over to God, or a higher spirit, to serve as guide. Sam had still not taken these steps. In Dan's experience, the more you worked the steps, the more spiritual you became, the better you got; everyone noticed the difference in you. But Sam, while baptized a Catholic, showed no sign of believing in or surrendering to a higher power; spirituality did not seem to be in him. Occasionally he expressed anger about his addiction, but that was it. He had encouraged Sam to work towards some of the other steps: for example, undertaking an honest "moral inventory" of himself, to write a form of confession, get it down on paper, and then admit to one other person and a higher power the nature of the wrongs committed. Sam

Pirrera would not conduct that inventory or admit his sins to himself, much less to another person, or God.

Dan gave Sam a ride after the meeting, as always, to a drop-off point several blocks away from his parents' home on Cannon Street, but not in front of any particular house. He was used to Sam not saying much after meetings. But tonight he seemed even quieter than usual.

"Have you started writing yet?"

"Not yet."

"What are you going to do now, are you working on yourself?"

"Yeah."

Sam got out of the parked truck, and Dan drove away. He would always wonder about that night, and his dealings with Sam, and whether he could have done more. Much later, his own NA sponsor would tell him he couldn't have done anything; how could Dan have known what Sam Pirrera was capable of?

* * *

Becky Hunter continued to work behind the bar at Pete's downtown. One day she saw a blond woman come through the door. She was relieved to see that it was Danielle. She was OK after all. They caught up. Becky had recently gone through some tough times in her personal life, but things were looking up.

"I'm back with my husband," Becky said.

"There's no chance of that for me," Danielle said. "My husband's been arrested."

Becky had known that Danielle's last name was Pirrera, but had not put it together before who her husband was. Now she knew. It was Sam Pirrera. She had seen his name in *The Hamilton Spectator*, read that he had been arrested in the case of body parts found in the garbage at his house. Danielle's *husband*?

Danielle told Becky the details of what she had seen and heard on Easter weekend, on Saturday, April 3. Sometime before 1 p.m. that day, Danielle had received a phone call. She heard that Sam was in his house on Burns Place, and she should get up there immediately. The person on the phone was Sam's mother, Lina Pirrera. Sam was losing control, talking about killing himself: he needed to get to a hospital.

Soon after 1 p.m., Danielle drove to her estranged husband's house, along with their toddler daughter. Lina Pirrera's car was in the driveway at 12 Burns Place. Danielle parked, looked around for a moment, then carried the baby in the car seat in the front door. Inside the house she saw Sam. He was wearing white and blue shorts with a Corona beer logo on them and a white T-shirt. He was on the couch, curled into a fetal position, sobbing, shaking. Broken dishes were everywhere.

Nearly two hours later, at 3 p.m., Sam and Danielle emerged from the house and got into Sam's white Cougar, Danielle behind the wheel. She drove him down the Mountain, to St. Joseph's Hospital. Not long after Sam and Danielle left, a neighbour watched as Sam's mother also exited the house, with the toddler, got in her car and drove away very slowly. She kept looking back at the house, almost as if it was the last time she was going to see it. And then a couple of minutes later, she drove back into Burns Place, full circle around the cul-de-sac, again staring at the house, and left once again.

Danielle checked Sam into the ER at the hospital. She sat in the waiting room with him, his head resting on her lap, stroking his hair. He told Danielle he had been bingeing on crack all week. At the hospital he was referred for crisis intervention treatment. Danielle got up to leave. She was heading

out when a nurse called her back. Your husband wants to tell
you something, the nurse said. Danielle returned to Sam in
the waiting area.

"I killed someone," he said.

"What?"

"This week."

"What are you talking about?"

"I'm tired of everyone f----n' leaving me so I killed someone. Picked up a hooker, we did some crack. She said she
wanted to leave. I told her she wasn't going anywhere. Got
rid of the body parts. All that's left is the guts and they're in
the garbage bag and box at the side of the house. I need you
to get rid of them for me."

Danielle left the hospital, picked up a girlfriend en route
to Burns Place. She parked outside the house, went inside,
and called 911. Even with the fear Sam had sown in Danielle
through their relationship, this time she had not followed
his directions, had not kept another secret. Up at the house,
Hamilton Police Constable Kathy Stewart pulled up and talked
to Danielle, she told Stewart that she had noticed strange
clothes, a woman's clothes, inside the house, along with broken pieces of furniture, a real mess. But, Danielle said, the
basement had recently been cleaned—"really cleaned." And
Sam never cleaned anything, she said.

"Do you think he is capable of killing someone?" Stewart
asked Danielle.

"Yes."

And then Stewart examined the bag at the side of the
house, discovered the body parts, called for backup, the investigation was on. That evening, detectives interviewed Danielle
at length. Her statement about what she saw and heard became
a crucial narrative for the investigation. But Danielle also knew
much more than what she told detectives that day.

* * *

*Sunday, April 4, 1999*
*5 p.m.*
*Central Station interview room*

Detective Sergeant Peter Abi-Rashed continued to work on Sam Pirrera in the interview room. Sam had no idea what, if anything, Danielle had told police.

"Did you have a guest visit Thursday or Friday?" Abi-Rashed asked.

"No," Sam said.

"You didn't have a guest?"

"My mother?"

"Sam."

"No. I didn't."

"Sam."

"No one."

"You know what?" Abi-Rashed said. "I thought that, back in the eighties, I didn't think I ever screwed you around. Did I? I did what I had to do, and you did what you had to do. And sometimes I caught you, and sometimes you got away. But this time, I've caught you. Don't you think? Sam? We've been in your house. If nothing happened in that house, if you didn't do anything, someone must have done something in that house and left that bag and box outside. I'm not going to beat around the bush. Who did you pick up?"

"Ask anyone on the street if I had anyone come to my house."

"Well, that's why I'm asking you, because I know you did."

"I didn't."

"You picked up someone."

"No, I didn't."

"OK, who was in your house, then?"

"Nobody. Maybe if I picked someone up I wouldn't have been so alone maybe."

"We went through what you did last week. Basically you said you were there all week, Monday freebasing, and Wednesday your parents came over. You were upset about your separation from your wife. Thursday nobody came to visit you. Friday nobody came to visit you. What were you doing yesterday?"

"I was freebasing a lot of cocaine and I called my wife and asked her to take me to St. Joe's to get help. I was attempting to hurt myself."

"So then what happened?"

"She told me everything was going to be all right, and the next thing I know you guys are banging on me."

"Banging on you? What do you mean?"

"Saying something about murder."

"Do you remember telling Danielle about, you know, 'taking out the garbage' at the side of the house?"

"No."

"Do you remember when Danielle picked you up and took you to the hospital Saturday? Don't agree with me if you don't agree with me. Do you remember that?"

"Yes."

"Do you remember asking her to do you a favor?"

"No."

"Sam—*Sam*. You asked her to do a favor and not tell anyone."

"No."

"Yeah. You asked her to do you a favor because you did something really stupid. She was supposed to go back to the house, Burns Place, and pick up a bag and a box by the side of the house. Starting to ring a bell here?"

Sam's chin was hanging, his eyes focused on the ground.

"Sam? Sam? Look at me," Abi-Rashed said. "You know I'm not making this up. I know you know."

"Well, somebody's making it up."

"Sam, we found what's in the bag and the box."

"What's in there?"

"You're going to dispute that?"

"I know nothing about that."

"So why would we end up at your house, looking in a bag and box and find this? Of all the homes in the city, we decide to go to Sam's house, and find a bag and a box, and look inside. And lo and behold! We find something that was left over from something that went very wrong. Look at me, Sam. Look at me. You're saying I'm wrong?"

"That's all I remember."

"Look, something pretty horrific happened in that house. You're upset, you're depressed. You're venting your frustrations, smashed up your own house, right? Used a baseball bat. Look at me, Sam. Do you agree with me, you're pretty upset, pretty pissed off?"

"Yeah."

"And why couldn't that carry over to you being pissed off at someone who is at your house?"

"I don't remember anyone else being at my house."

In a room across the hall from Abi-Rashed, Detective Mark Petkoff monitored the questioning on a monitor, and typed suggested questions on his laptop that Abi-Rashed read on a teleprompter built in to the surface of his desk.

"You were on a bender, you're all by yourself, you went back to coke and crack, using them as a crutch. Is that right?" Abi-Rashed asked.

"Yeah."

"And you have someone who comes to help you, and what you were trying to do is lose yourself, Sam. Trying to separate yourself into two Sams, and freebasing was helping you do that. And no one wanted to help you. Sam, look at me. It wasn't you that did those things in your house, it was your loneliness that caused you to do this."

Abi-Rashed's voice, rising. "Sam! Look at me! Do you agree with me?"

"I don't believe I killed anybody, OK? So I don't know what you're talking about."

"Well, Sam, you know what the problem is? You can't stand someone leaving you. Do you agree with me?"

"Yeah?"

"Sam, talk to me. Why are we going around in circles here?"

"I told you I don't want to talk about it any more."

"I see. Do you have nightmares?"

"No."

"No nightmares, Sam? Look at me. You picked up someone, right? You're already hurting. Nobody there for support, nobody cares about Sam. You don't know what to do, you're freebasing, you try to kill that loneliness, that 'nobody cares' feeling. You get someone back to your house. Sam, look at me. You do some coke with her, you have a bit of fun, feeling better, but then it's time for her to leave, right? Sam? It's time for her to leave, right?"

"I don't know what you're talking about."

"You're going to be lonely, once she leaves you're back to being lonely. And Sam doesn't like being lonely. 'Cause it hurts. So you stop her. And then you realize, 'Oh my God, what did I do?' And now you realize: 'I've got to cover up. Clean up. This didn't happen.' Right?"

# CHAPTER 9 ~ MISSING PIECES

Detective Mark Petkoff, observing on the monitor, thought that Sam was definitely a player. He knew what he was doing. Very evasive. And he was a hard-looking man, the look he possessed, if there was such a thing as an evil stare, Sam had it. Petkoff had worked vice and drugs, where you see your share of addicts, and they have that look, that drained expression, that walking dead look that shows they are on the crack diet. But Sam, for all his crack abuse, he didn't have that same look. Looked rough after being in lockup, certainly, but didn't look as bad as many of the addicts he had seen. And, while he evaded Abi-Rashed's questions, Sam didn't also didn't seem all that worried. Arrogant, if anything, a nonchalance to his answers. And he was sticking to a real simple storyline.

Petkoff had an idea for turning up the volume a bit. Time to play the ex-wife card. He typed in a new question for Abi-Rashed.

"Remember Beverly?" Abi-Rashed asked Sam, referencing Sam's first wife.

"Beverly?" Sam said. "What about her?"

"She wanted to leave, too."

"Yeah, she's gone. She's dancing."

"Dancing? Where did she go?"

"What do you mean? She was dancing in California, I guess. I don't know. What's Beverly got to do with this?"

"Well, you were happy with Beverly, right?"

"Yes."

"But she wasn't happy with the relationship, right?"

"I guess."

"And she wanted to leave?"

"Yeah."

"Didn't that hurt you?"

"Sure, a bit."

"And you can't bear that, you can't stand that a woman would leave you. Beverly left you, right? And now Danielle leaves you, you can't stand that, being alone. And now you have a girl in your place, she's making you feel a bit better, and what happens, Sam? She wants to leave."

"She left."

Abi-Rashed pounced. Sam had finally admitted that a woman was in his house.

"She left?"

"I told you guys I don't want to talk about this any more."

"What do you mean she left, she left out the door?"

"She left out the door."

"Why couldn't you tell me that in the first place?"

"Which?"

"That she left out the door. You said she left. Where did she go?"

"Out on the street, I guess."

"Where did you pick her up?"

"Do you remember what I said about a half-hour ago? I don't want to say any more."

"OK. How did she end up at your house?"

"She didn't."

"You just said she left your house."

"You keep putting words in my mouth. Now I don't want to say no more, please."

"I'm not putting words in your mouth, Sam. The girl you had in your house, did she have red hair?"

"I don't know."

"You don't know? But she left your house, though? What time did she leave your house?"

"Three in the morning, I think."

"How was she going to get back?"

"Cab."

Gary Yokoyama

Detective Mark Petkoff.

"Did she call a cab from your place?"

"Yes."

"What was her first name?"

"I don't know. We didn't talk about names."

"What did you guys do?"

"Just blast."

"Blast? What's blast?"

"Coke."

"Where did you meet her?"

"Just walking down the Mountain, I guess."

"What? She's walking down the Mountain? Where down the Mountain? It's a big Mountain."

"By Upper Wellington, I guess. I asked if she needed a ride. I don't want to talk any more."

"So you're on Upper Wellington, you see this girl, you offer her a ride. Did you know her?"

"No. Never seen her before. I said, 'Do you want to party?' So we smoked some coke and that was it."

"Then she called a cab and left?"

"Yes."

"Did you see her get in the cab?"

"Yes."

"What kind?"

"Yellow."

"What time?"

"Three."

"I might be a little confused here, but what day was that now?"

"Could have been like Thursday. I don't keep track of all these days and times."

"OK Sam, this is pretty important. You are alone, for the past six weeks, feeling pretty shitty, no one coming around, no one cares. You are freebasing coke pretty good in that last week. Nobody cares about Sam. Finally you find someone who will talk to Sam, and party with Sam. Pick her up, a bit of basing, and then something goes wrong. Right, Sam?"

Sam said nothing.

"She wanted to leave, Sam."

"She left."

"She didn't leave, Sam."

"I don't want to talk to you no more."

"She didn't leave, Sam."

"Did you hear me?"

"She didn't leave, Sam—you were upset she was leaving. No one is going to leave you any more. You are having a good time, freebasing, feel a bit better, and now she wants to leave. She didn't leave—did she?"

"She left."

"She didn't leave, because we found parts of her outside your house. Sam, she didn't leave, did she?"

"She left."

"The only way she left was in bags and boxes. We've got doctors that examined what we found at your house, we know what went on in that house. When she said she had to leave you, you snapped. Sam, you couldn't put up with it. Could you? Did you?"

He said nothing.

"Then she said, 'I want out of here', and you said: 'No way, you're stayin'. Nobody leaves here.' You got pissed off at her."

"I said twenty minutes ago I didn't want to say no more," Sam said.

Sam gestured toward the Canadian Charter of Rights caution card that Abi-Rashed had on the desk, the card that said he didn't have to talk if he didn't want to.

"Is that lying f-----g bullshit on that piece of paper then? I can stop anytime I want. I don't want to talk no more."

"Sam," Abi-Rashed said, voice calm, "you don't have to say anything, but I can sit here for hours. I can talk as long as I want. Now, Sam, where will we find the rest of her?"

"The rest of who? What are you talking about? I have no idea."

The interview concluded at 6 p.m. An hour and a half, and Abi-Rashed had made some progress. Sam admitted that there had been a woman in his home during the critical time period—a day or two before body parts were found. But he had admitted nothing further. He was about to be moved from Central Station lockup to Barton Street jail, to await his first appearance in court. He would soon be meeting with his lawyer. The window for police talking to him would probably close. Still, Abi-Rashed planned to approach him again down the road, when Sam Pirrera's head was clearer, and his options more stark.

* * *

Homicide detectives turn to the media when they are missing critical pieces of the puzzle. That was certainly the case here and Peter Abi-Rashed knew it.

*The Hamilton Spectator*
*Monday April 5, 1999*
*Cops scour neighborhood for missing body parts*

Police began scouring a city neighborhood for human body parts following the arrest of a man for first-degree murder on Saturday. Body parts were found in a bag inside a box at a city home, but police said that "significant portions" of the body are missing. Police are asking that anyone with information about the homicide or about "any recent missing person" should call them at 540-5500 or Crime Stoppers at 522-TIPS.

There is always a steady flow of missing person reports filed with Hamilton Police, but now they increased dramatically. On Monday morning, Detective Wayne Bennett was called down to the front desk at Central Station. A man met Bennett and said he was worried that he had not heard from his sister. The last name was Karer. He described her: brown eyes, long dark hair. And her lifestyle had at times been a high-risk one. The man said he hadn't seen his sister in a week, not since March 28. She hadn't come to Easter dinner as planned. No, she did not lead the most predictable life, but skipping out on a family dinner without a word was not her way. His sister's name was Maggie.

* * *

*1968*
*Hamilton*

The long chestnut brown hair framed the little girl's face, her nose pressed against the front door window, waiting, waiting, and then the face broke into a smile. Daddy's huge frame unfolded as he got out of the car, home from work at the factory. The little girl's name was Margaret, but everyone called her Maggie. A perfect smile, her mother used to say, her face is so beautiful: *"My Maggie, my Maggie."*

Maggie's parents, Les and Margaret, grew up in Hungary in the 1940s, and in 1957 emigrated to Canada, refugees of the bloody Hungarian Revolution. Les Karer settled in Northern Ontario, working in the mines in Timmins, and later moved to Hamilton. He was over six feet tall, dark hair, a strong, imposing, man. For a time he worked as a professional wrestler on weekends. There was a family photo, black and white, Les in his wrestler's jumpsuit, in the ready position, an intense look on his face, the strong jaw, darkly handsome, flat stomach, big arms. Not a body builder's physique, but the naturally big hard body of a working man: a giant.

Les met Margaret at a Hungarian community dance in Hamilton. They married in 1961 and Margaret gave birth to a son in 1962. She desperately yearned for a girl, and on September 22, 1964, Maggie was born at 2 a.m. at St. Joseph's Hospital, a quick delivery. The nurse looked at all that dark hair and dark eyes. "A pretty girl," she said, and the Karers beamed. The family lived at 31 Bobolink Road on the central Mountain, back in the days when that was the distant southern edge of Hamilton's sprawl. Neighborhood kids were intimidated by Mr. Karer when they first laid eyes on him, but, although he was a disciplinarian, he was like a big friendly bear, always waving to everyone, a big smile on his face. Maggie was the beautiful princess, Daddy's Little Girl.

Young Maggie with her brother.

Maggie attended Cardinal Heights Elementary School from kindergarten to Grade 8. One of her best friends was Kim Mcgilvery, who lived nearby. The two girls played when they were younger, with Barbies, skipping, hopscotch, listening to music. Maggie loved Billy Joel, the Beatles, Supertramp. She would join in singing to match the group's high-pitched melodies. They hung out at Cardinal Variety off Bobolink and skated at the old Mountain Arena, catching the circus when it came to town. Kim walked over to the Karers' house; it was always immaculately clean, and there were the familiar smells: Mr. Karer's cured meats, bacon in the cellar, and Mrs. Karer constantly cooking and baking in the kitchen, having plucked green and red peppers and jalapenos from the garden. Les Karer gave Kim a hug. He was that kind of man; she loved him.

In 1977, the Karers moved a few blocks southwest to Maitland Avenue. Upstairs in the split-level home, the first bedroom on the right was Maggie's: wood-frame bed was a large dresser with three-paneled mirror. And above the bed, was a small painting, a girl with black hair and a red hair band, a profile from the side, the eyes turned as though sneaking a peek, a trace of a grin on her mouth.

In her early teens, with high school at Hill Park looming, Maggie had grown to be five-foot-eight—a tall, beautiful girl. One summer's day, before the new world of Grade 9 began, a girl named Maria Barone was hanging around the Fortinos supermarket on Limeridge Road West. That's where she met Maggie Karer for the first time. Maria was struck by the hair—all the girls were. It flowed down to the middle of her back; in summer it turned a golden brown. And Maggie's skin, especially in summer, had a slight olive cast to it. That summer Maggie started to come over and hang with Maria and the others. Maggie always wore jeans, or jean shorts, and running shoes. They shot hoops on the basket in the driveway and played 21. Maggie was pretty athletic. Her personality was understated: she had a shy grin, and quiet giggle.

Photo courtesy of the author

Maggie Karer as a teen.

The back yard at Maria's place was huge; they did gymnastics, cartwheels. They picked fruit right off the trees—apples, peaches—or from the boysenberry bush. The girls lay down in the back yard on the grass, looking up into the sky, Maggie's olive skin warming in the sun. They talked—about boys, anything and everything. Maggie spoke of her dreams. Early evening, when the light drained from the sky, Maggie had to go home. Her parents' traditional values kept her on a strict curfew. She wasn't allowed to stay out past 8 p.m. At dusk, Maria and her sister walked Maggie home.

Maggie wanted to get married and have a big family. Maybe be a model someday. Weren't the girls always telling her how beautiful her hair was, and her smile? Or maybe a nurse, make a good living, support her mother financially. Mom worked so hard in her cleaning job.

"One day, Mom, I'm going to make enough money, you can just relax," she told her.

Starting high school in the fall offered Maggie new possibilities and choices. Her childhood friend Kim had already started at Hill Park. Kim was a follower, yearned to be accepted. She got in with who she thought was the cool gang. She loved walking the hallways with them, crowds parting at the sight of the group. The power of it was intoxicating. So were the drugs the group was doing: hash, oil, pot.

Maggie fell in with the same crowd. She was pretty and personable. She still kept in touch with Maria Barone, although Maria went to a different school. Maria would drive her dad's big brown Ford LTD to meet Maggie during a spare to grab a smoke. Maggie introduced her new friends. A tough group of girls, Maria thought. Maggie seemed to be able to fit in with any crowd. Too pretty to be considered butchy, she had developed a confidence about her that fit in with the cool tough girls as well.

"Wow, your friends—how can you hang out with them?" Maria said.

"They're good to me," Maggie replied.

Maggie started challenging her parents' rules, flouting her curfews. One night, Maggie said she was going to a friend's house. Her father secretly followed her in the car. In fact she went somewhere else, to one of the bad girls' homes. Big Les Karer took Maggie to task for it. Some friends believed the Maggie they knew was an independent spirit who did her own thing; she was never a follower. But her mother felt there were a couple of girls who had egged Maggie on to abuse drugs, who had poisoned her mind.

Her father held out hope that if Maggie was exposed to different people and experiences, it would be good for her, change her perspective. He planned a summer trip for the whole family back to their roots, to Hungary. But if drugs and the wrong people were changing Maggie's life, and not for the better, an event one winter day in 1982 changed her world, and, some believed, perhaps her destiny.

Her father went to play the horses at Flamboro Downs, a track outside Hamilton. He drove home along Highway 6, a portion of which always screamed with heavy truck traffic and speeding cars; a route infamous for automobile accidents. The roads were especially bad that day—icy. He was in a head-on collision and died. The news shattered Maggie. She was 17 years old. Her father had been old school, but she had a special relationship with him. He had tried to keep her in his big-armed, protective embrace, and now he was gone. She cried a lot, would talk to Kim about it a bit, but around her family, including her older brother, she mostly kept to herself about it. She felt anger at God for taking him away.

The summer after Les died, the family decided to still take the trip he had been planning. He would have wanted that.

Photo courtesy of the author

Young Maggie with her Mom and Dad.

They headed to Budapest in July. Maggie loved it. In fact, her brother and mother returned to Canada but Maggie stayed on in Hungary, rooming with her aunt for six months. She felt a strong connection with the place. She wouldn't stop talking about it when she returned—the food, the warm, laid-back people, all the history. Maybe she felt closer to

her father in the old country. She dreamt of him. She told
her mom about it.

"It was so clear; I could see Daddy. And he said to me,
'Maggie, are you happy?' And I said, 'Yes, I'm happy.'"

Maybe if she had, somehow, been able to stay in Hungary
just a little longer, maybe just a year, enough time to make
other connections, start down new paths, it would have made
a difference. Instead, the trip exists in Maggie Karer's life like
a fantasy. She returned to Hamilton and a life that she had
chosen or perhaps by now had chosen her. It was a life that
would soon take her from the rough crowd at Hill Park high
school to the rougher crowd of the lower city. Ultimately, it
would lead her to Sam Pirrera.

# Chapter 10 ~ "We've Got Another One"

*Monday, April 5, 1999*
*12 Burns Place*
*9:30 a.m.*

Peter Abi-Rashed met in the Hamilton Police command van outside Sam Pirrera's house with forensic detectives Ross Wood, Gary Zwicker and Curt Napholc to review the game plan for the search. Ident would go room by room, catalogue evidence, obtain swabs from objects for DNA samples to compare with DNA from the body parts found in the garbage, and also with DNA profiles of missing people on file with police. They would start at the front of the story-and-a-half house, photographing and videotaping as they went. It was essential that the integrity of the scene be maintained, Abi-Rashed said. Simply moving an item of clothing or a broken dish from its original position could be cited by a defense lawyer as altering the crime scene. If the scene was compromised in any way, they could then lose all evidence they found from that point forward.

And yet their mission was also to leave no stone unturned. This was six years after the Bernardo investigation, in which police searching the killer's home in St. Catharines had infamously failed to find crucial videotapes behind a ceiling panel. Ross Wood and his forensic team heard the directions loud and clear. They had no idea what they'd find, but nothing would be left to chance. If there was evidence in that house, anywhere, they would find it. This could not be another Bernardo.

"Tear the place apart if you have to," one of the detectives told the Ident officers. "Do what you have to do."

A house search is a laborious process that can take several days. Put down floor covering so there is no contamination, videotape and photograph everything, take notes, gather exhibits. In a neat and clean house, the search is simplified considerably. But much of Sam Pirrera's house was a shambles, broken dishes everywhere, broken furniture. Everything was potential evidence. If they never found the rest of the body, the smallest trace of the victim's presence might make or break the case. They had to collect individual bits of broken glass to dust for fingerprints, swab marks on walls that might be traces of blood.

Ident tent at 12 Burns Place.

Ident started on the main floor, in the living room and kitchen, which took more than a day, before moving upstairs, searching square foot by square foot. They took plates off electrical sockets to check in the cavities behind. A weapon could be there, anything. Upstairs in a closet, they found a piece of plywood covering an entrance to the attic. A hiding place. Insulation in behind? Gary Zwicker, the new guy in Ident, figured he'd get tapped for that job, and soon enough he was sweaty and itchy from ripping up insulation.

Ident detectives gather and process evidence: their role is not to develop a narrative of the case, or speculate on the motive of a killer. But given the nature of this case, a likely murder and dismemberment, certain items in the house caught the eye. Among the books found were *The Last Dance: Murder in Canada*; *The Collected Works of Max Haines*; *Unfinished Murder: The Capture of a Serial Rapist*; and *Lethal Marriage: The Story of Paul Bernardo and Karla Homolka*. The detectives talked about it. What if the remains found so far were just the beginning? What if they were dealing with more than one body? They might be on the trail of a serial killer.

That afternoon, Peter Abi-Rashed worked at his desk in the Major Crime office at Central Station. On the wall behind him hung a framed drawing of a uniformed cop, the cap shading the unknown officer's face, a darkened city skyline in the background. An old friend gave it to him a long time ago when he first got on as a cop. He kept it at home for a while, then decided to bring it to the office, where it hung among plaques and citations. Abi-Rashed had acquired his share of recognition for his investigative work, even though his personality suggested that he cared not at all for such things. He seemed more concerned with talking visitors into buying a chocolate bar for the latest charitable cause on his plate.

It was still very early days in the J. Doe case. He tried to stay positive; it was too early to be getting discouraged that they still didn't have a full body, or even a crime scene. Conventional wisdom is that you need the victim's body to get a murder conviction. But Abi-Rashed knew otherwise. He had worked a dismemberment before, the Julie Stanton case in 1994. He was part of Project Hitchhiker, the Ontario provincial task force investigating her disappearance and death. Hamilton's Peter Stark was charged with drugging the teenage girl (who had been from the Pickering area, near Toronto) murdering her with an axe and dismembering and hiding the body. Police had not recovered the body but Stark was convicted for the crime anyway. It wasn't until after the trial that the body parts were found in a wooded area.

Abi-Rashed had plenty of other work on the go. The preliminary hearing in the Baby Maliek case was coming up in a couple of weeks, the critical step in getting their case against Maliek's mother, Carmelita Willie, and her boyfriend, Carlos Clarke, to court for trial. Abi-Rashed knew they had staked out unusual ground in law enforcement with that one, charging two people with the death of a 14-month-old child. The Crown was trying to prosecute the boyfriend with murder for beating the little boy to death over a period of eight days, and the mother for manslaughter for letting it happen. Typically you don't charge both caregivers with the death of a child. Abi-Rashed heard colleagues say it couldn't be done, that there was no way they'd get both parties to trial, much less win a double conviction, but then he was the type who relished such skepticism. They were going for it all.

At 1:46 p.m., his phone rang.

"Abi-Rashed. Major Crime."

It was with respect to the J. Doe case, he was told, another report of a possible missing person responding to the police request for tips. There was a woman in the lobby downstairs. Her name was Lesa Davidson.

"Yeah?"

The name didn't ring a bell with him.

"How long has the person been missing?" Abi-Rashed asked the officer on the phone.

"Eight years."

*Eight years? 1991? What the —*

"OK," he sighed. "Have her come up."

He met the woman in an interview room near his office. He introduced himself and they sat down.

"I'm Lesa Davidson," she said, in a thickly French-flavored accent. "I want to report that my daughter has been missing for eight years."

"What is your daughter's name?"

"Beverly. She used to be married to Sam Pirrera."

Abi-Rashed felt a shiver. *Beverly.*

He knew well the best predictor of a criminal's behavior is his past. The perp repeats successes and avoids mistakes. He remembered what Sam had said during the interrogation. *"She's gone. Beverly's dancing in California, I guess."*

Abi-Rashed looked at Mrs. Davidson, his expression flat, even as his heart raced.

"Ah, yes, ma'am, wait here, I'll be—I'll be right back. OK?"

He closed the door, and saw Detective Mark Petkoff in the corridor.

"Holy shit," Abi-Rashed said. "We've got another one."

* * *

Lesa Denechaud was from Quebec City, one of seven children. She married an English Canadian man in Montreal named Doug Davidson. Early in the marriage they moved to Toronto, where Doug worked driving a truck. On August 29, 1969, after a 15-hour labor, Lesa gave birth to their first child, a brown-eyed girl. They named her Beverly Ann, after Doug's sister, but called her Bev. Fifteen months after Bev was born, Lesa gave birth to a boy, Douglas Jr. The family lived in a small, two-bedroom apartment. Bev was a quiet baby, spoiled like a first child. As a little girl she loved wearing princess dresses, and later was inseparable from her cat, a black one named Midnight.

Young Bev Davidson.

The family moved to Hamilton, where Bev attended Wentworth Street School in the east end for kindergarten to Grade 5, then Tweedsmuir for Grades 6 to 8. She was a bright girl, but did not have strong education role models to follow; her mother only made it to Grade 9, her father Grade 8. Bev had close friends, girls like her best friend Karen, and hung out with her brother Doug. As a teenager she colored her light brown hair blond. At five-foot-six, she was slim and attractive. She had a bubbly personality, was popular but also had an independent streak and did not bend to peer pressure on smoking, drinking, or drugs. She hung with Karen, shopping, trying on clothes, rarely buying anything because they didn't have any money. They did silly stuff, had a thing for eating hot banana peppers straight out of a jar. In summer, they sunbathed on Burlington Beach on Lake Ontario.

But Bev's life was about to be dominated by a boy who started to demand, and receive, her attention. In 1984, the Davidsons moved to a house in Hamilton's east end, called Adams Street, an abbreviated dead-end street running south off busy Cannon. The teenage boy lived right across Cannon and had a clear view from his attic bedroom window of the Davidson place, where he could keep an eye out for the pretty 15-year-old girl.

Before long, the small dark-haired teenage boy came calling for Bev. He knocked on the front door at 9 Adams. Lesa Davidson opened it and, with his usual bluntness, he asked for her daughter, did not say hello to Mrs. Davidson, did not call her by name, did not look her in the eye. His name was Sam Pirrera. Lesa noticed how Sam had this way of looking at her but away from her at the same time, his eyes tilting

Gary Yokoyama

Sam and Bev's old neighborhood.

downward. Was that shyness? Arrogance? It bothered her. And pretty soon he stopped knocking at the door at all. He would phone the house and tell Bev to meet him outside, and out she would go.

Lesa believed Sam's parents, Lina and Antonio Pirrera, were also opposed to the relationship. But for the Pirreras, she believed, it was because Bev was not Italian. Bev never seemed to set foot in the Pirrera house. As for Lesa, she did not trust Sam from the first time she met him. It wasn't just about being a protective mother; it was simply the first impression he left. It was his manner, his eyes, and the fact that he seemed to be taking over Bev's life. Her attention was entirely focused on him, even to the exclusion of her school work.

Bev was a popular girl, and there was another neighborhood boy who had a crush on her. Bev liked him, but only as a friend. She only seemed to have eyes for Sam. Why was that? Her friend Karen figured it was probably Sam's bad boy appeal. He wasn't a particularly handsome guy, although he did dress well. Lesa thought he was unattractive, although that was probably more an extension of his cocky, sarcastic vibe. Bev did feel that Sam was a good listener, at least early in their relationship, which was good for her; she was going through a lot at home, not getting along well with her mother or her father. When Bev was 12, she had run away because of the family situation. Sam provided an ear for her, and Sam, in turn, shared his anxiety about problems in his own family.

The fault lines in Sam's personality were not helped by his growing experimentation with drugs. He dabbled in marijuana, although that wasn't unusual for a teenage boy back then. But casual use became regular use. By the time he was 17, he was addicted to crack cocaine. He also started to have run-ins with police. He was convicted of minor theft, driving offences, and drug possession. Still he continued to date Bev, they started talking about getting married, even though Bev hadn't even turned 17.

It became increasingly difficult for Lesa to monitor the relationship, and it didn't help that things were not good between Lesa and her husband Doug. He wasn't home much and their marriage was nearing an end. She was holding down three cleaning jobs, working shifts. She would go to work early in the morning to clean schools, come home, then back out at night to the next job to clean doctors' offices, and get home around midnight. Often, when she left her house at night and crossed Cannon, she would see Sam upstairs in the Pirrera house, staring out his bedroom window. She could swear he was grinning at her. She knew he was just waiting for her to leave; then he would meet up with Bev so they could go to the Wentworth Street school yard nearby.

Lesa gave it to Sam straight one day.

"I don't like you being around my daughter," she said in her thick French accent. "I don't trust you."

Sam just grinned back at her and said nothing. Lesa burned. The look was like a slap in the face. Sam reeked of that "screw-you" attitude. He did not just go against Lesa's

Gary Yokoyama

The Davidson's house on Adams Street.

wishes, he did so brazenly, although he hated interference from both families. Day and night, out his bedroom window, Sam trumpeted his love for Bev loud enough for all to hear. One of the pop standards of the day was Phil Collins' "Against All Odds."

*How can I just let you walk away, just let you leave without a trace*

*When I stand here taking every breath with you, ooh?*

*You're the only one who really knew me at all.*

*So take a look at me now, oh there's just an empty space,*

*And you coming back to me is against the odds and that's what I've got to face.*

"How can I just let you walk away, just let you leave without a trace"—simply overwrought love song lyrics, but ones that would take on dark meaning in Beverly Davidson's life with Sam Pirrera.

# CHAPTER 11 ~ MONSTER

*Wednesday, April 7, 1999*
*Central Station*

At the daily morning meeting on the J. Doe case, Peter Abi-Rashed met with a detective who had been transferred out of child abuse section to homicide to join the investigating team. His name was Dave Place. At six-foot-five and 220 pounds, with bulging arms, Place looked the most like a cop of any of them. But he also came across soft-spoken and cerebral. Abi-Rashed explained the new angle in the Pirrera investigation. It was Sam Pirrera's ex-wife, Beverly, maiden name Davidson.

Abi-Rashed looked at Dave Place.

"You need to find Beverly Davidson or prove that she's dead," he said.

Place wrote down the directive. He was excited about getting on board his first case in homicide, his first big caper, as he called it. He decided that the approach he would take would start from the assumption that Beverly was alive, somewhere, and he needed to gather information that would lead him to her.

Two days later, on Friday, April 9, the forensic search inside Sam Pirrera's house on Burns Place moved into its fifth day. The Ident team had started on the main floor, then gone upstairs, and back down again, videotaping, photographing, tagging, and bagging potential evidence. There was one level left to check. That day, detectives Ross Wood, Gary Zwicker, and Curt Napholc made it into the basement. From the first night, when he got a quick look at the inside of the house, Wood had a sense that something was odd in the basement. The rest of the house was a disaster—broken furniture, smashed dishes, clothes strewn everywhere. But the basement was clean, even smelled of disinfectant. And he had noticed an inordinate number of flies down there as well.

Woody was 52 years old, on the job 35 years, and nearing the end of the line in his career, although at this point he was still not thinking about retirement. An officer had once told him, when the time is right, you'll know. He had wanted to be a cop since he was five years old. His goal had been to be a Mountie, and he worked for the Royal Canadian Mounted Police for four years at the start of his law enforcement career.

In his nine years in Ident division with Hamilton Police, he had been lead forensic investigator in two dozen homicide cases. His cool, understated personality helped him cope with the blood and guts and tragedy that were a regular part of working Ident. But his mind and heart were not entirely immune. One case that stuck with him happened a few years before he was assigned Pirrera. It was the case where a mother, her daughter and son had been stabbed to death in their home in Stoney Creek, just east of Hamilton. Lots of blood. They photographed and gathered evidence around three bodies. It was tough to take. On the job, like the other Ident officers, Wood leaned on black humor. Some guys looked at you like you were sick or weird, but you had to find a way to talk about it openly, release the tension, or it would drive you crazy.

How did he deal with crime scenes where bodies were badly decomposed, the stench unbearable?

"At a distance."

And Wood, for one, also relied heavily on his wife, Marjory, for support. Marjory was a nurse at Hamilton General Hospital, who worked in the intensive care unit. She saw her share of tragedy, too. She was his sounding board, his debriefing session, and she understood. It also helped to stay as detached from the victims as possible. You need tunnel vision on the job. Collect evidence and preserve it. Don't think about the victim or suspect. That's for the Major Crime detectives.

At a scene, Wood didn't want to know who the people were. He didn't have much choice with the Stoney Creek stabbing case, though. At that time, somebody in the police service had decided there should be debriefing for officers involved. The thinking was that it would help them cope with the horror. So they called Wood and his partner, Frank Pedersen, off the scene back to the station for a chat. Wood, never one to let nonsense go uncontested, argued against it. But it was policy. At the debriefing they were told about the family, what had happened. It was the worst thing they could have done. The crime scene was no longer just a job; he knew more than he wanted to. The bodies had names. Personalities. Later the policy was changed: the debriefings became optional.

Gary Yokoyama

Ident detective Ross Wood.

Another case that stuck with him was one where three bodies were found after several days. Two of them were children. Wood was surprised; he had grown kids, but his partner, David Doel, had young children around the same age as the victims, and Doel handled it a lot better than he did. No matter how much Woody saw on the job, no matter how much he could detach himself, he never could take child victims. Adults do what they do to each other. But kids? They're just kids, he thought. They didn't do anything.

* * *

As they had with each room in Sam Pirrera's house, they laid down protective tarp in the basement, the rec room. Wood, Zwicker, and Napholc wore disposable white coveralls and masks. Without a mask, you could contaminate the scene if you sneezed or coughed, introducing DNA that hadn't been there before. There was the wall-to-wall dark red carpet with a black pattern in it; brown-padded stocked bar, wainscoting around the walls, mirror paneling on the walls. Full-size pool table in the middle, plastic covering on it, a full ashtray on top. Couple of pool cues on the floor, couple of children's dolls. Two bottles of Mr. Clean on the bar, one of them nearly empty. Someone had been doing some vigorous cleaning in that room.

The detectives were on the floor, rolling back portions of the tarp to examine the carpet, searching for clues, literally one square foot at a time, taking notes, videotaping, and taking photographs as they went, going slow. All they might hope to find was a wisp of hair, a fingernail. It was critical not to blow it. The basement was dimly lit. They used alternative light around the pool table that dominated the middle of the room—ultraviolet, white light, flashlights, different colors.

They searched on their hands and knees, eyes close against the wall, focusing.

Gary Yokoyama

Ident team Curt Napholc, Gary Zwicker, and Ross Wood.

"Woody. Got something over here."

It was Curt Napholc. He was shining intense white light near the baseboard above the red carpet, on the wood panel wainscoting, and below the pool cue rack. His eye focused on what looked like a minute piece of skin. Fine fibers attached, perhaps hair. And beside the bit of skin, a speck, a tiny dark speck. Blood? Napholc thought so, from a high-impact spatter, where blood is projected almost like a mist. It would come from someone who had been beaten with a blunt object.

Wood and Zwicker moved closer for a look. The location of the speck was interesting. If someone cuts their finger with a tool, for example, they bleed and clean up, but the blood will be higher up somewhere, on a table, a counter, a wall. But this skin and blood was low, right by the carpet. They continued looking. More high-impact spatter, down low by the floor. And still more blood. Ross Wood dialed on his cell. It was 4:15 p.m.

"Abi-Rashed."

"Abi—we have a scene."

Abi-Rashed's eyes lit up. Woody had spoken the four words that meant everything. They had hunches and hypotheses before. Now they had a crime scene, six days after the case began. Abi-Rashed checked a vehicle out of the Central Station garage, headed down King William, right on Wellington, and took the Sherman Access up the Mountain, his heart pounding. *We have a scene.*

At 4:35 p.m., Wood briefed Abi-Rashed and Detective Wayne Bennett on what they had just found in Sam Pirrera's rec room. After the briefing, Wood, Zwicker, and Napholc headed back to the basement to continue. They put down more floor covering and worked their way, again inch by inch, from the rec room to the unfinished fruit cellar portion of the basement.

It was cool in the cellar. They took the temperature: 48 degrees F. The room was cramped, about five feet by five feet. There was a white floor fan and a wooden stool. Another fan, another stool—no, it was the reflection of the fan and stool against the cellar wall. The wall had mirror paneling attached, taped on. A crude job. Why? And why have mirror panels on the wall of a fruit cellar?

By now it was just after 6 p.m. The detectives started to peel off the tape, and the mirror panels. The panels were not flush against the exterior wall; rather, they formed a false wall. And the false wall concealed a narrow space—not a room, just a space wide enough to hide something. And now they could see bags and boxes in the space.

Zwicker took photos, Wood made notes. Napholc opened a big green garbage bag. There was a cooler inside, like a two-handled cooler you'd take to the beach. Napholc moved the cooler closer to them. Photograph the cooler. Open the lid. Photograph the cooler with the lid open. There were packages inside, individually wrapped in layers of different types of materials—cloth, towels, garbage bags, a big comforter.

One of the packages was oval in shape. They carefully lifted it out of the cooler. Made a small incision with a knife in the thick wrapping, then peeled back a layer. And another layer. And another; peeled back just enough to reveal a small portion of what was concealed. And now they knew.

"We have a head. That's enough. Close it."

They left the house and briefed Abi-Rashed on the discovery. The three forensic detectives returned to the basement, sorted through more boxes, taking more photos. There were many more packages with multiple wrappings. More body parts. On re-entry to the basement, they now detected an odor that had not been noticeable before when they wore their masks, and before they had taken down the false-wall of mirrors in the cellar. The smell was gasoline. Where was it coming from? In the cellar, the detectives found their answer. It was the body parts. The packages had been dipped in accelerant. Gasoline. Why?

The cold room where the parts were found.

They took several trips carrying the containers from the cellar up the stairs, setting them inside a forensic services tent that had been set up on the front lawn. At 8:40 p.m. the body removal service van arrived. Just after 9 p.m. the van left for Hamilton General Hospital. Police must maintain continuity of all evidence in a homicide investigation. When it comes to a body, detectives fill out a log book to account for every minute the corpse is under their control. Peter Abi-Rashed got in his car and followed close behind the van when it pulled away. The company, called Great Lakes Removal, and police have a routine; visual contact must be maintained, the van doesn't run yellow lights. The two vehicles arrived at the hospital at 9:16 p.m.

The boxes and cooler were loaded on a gurney and wheeled down to the morgue in the basement and pushed into a security locker. Abi-Rashed logged it in. The remains

Hamilton Police Service

represented body No. 556 for 1999. That's how many bodies had been checked into the General's morgue so far that year — all deaths, homicides, or otherwise, from Hamilton and some neighboring jurisdictions. He labeled the remains "J. Doe" and noted that it was a Hamilton police homicide investigation, and that one person had been arrested. He locked the door and taped a forensic seal on it, writing down No. 1U20950, and the time, 9:30 p.m. He drove home for the night and carried the key with him into his house.

* * *

Criminal dismemberment is a rare event following a homicide. A criminal profiler who conducted a survey of 20,000 homicide cases found that about 100 could be said to involve dismemberment, or "criminal mutilation." Serial killers, too, rarely dismember, typically leaving the bodies, because the victims are usually strangers to the killer, and the murder usually has taken place in the victim's home; the killer leaves so there's no need to dismember and hide what he has done.

Dismemberment is, in some cases, termed "offensive" or "aggressive mutilation." Here the motivation varies, but the killer finds some perverse pleasure cutting the victim. Perhaps he is convinced that dismembering will cleanse the victim of an evil spirit. Serial killer Jeffrey Dahmer exhibited elements of necrophilia and cannibalism in dismembering his victims. In one case in Florida, a killer cut his victims because he was trying to satisfy an obsession with performing autopsies. He killed his mother, his wife, and his niece and dismembered all of them, before taking his own life.

But then there is dismemberment that profilers term a "defensive" action, where a killer who is driven to cover up his actions descends to an especially dark place. In general, forensic psychologists and criminal profilers say that when a killer tries to do something that will hide what he has done, to fool police, friends, and family, he is engaged in a rational act of sorts; in domestic homicides, some manner of defensive maneuver, or "scene staging," is attempted by the killer after the fact in 10 percent of the cases. Try to make the scene look like someone else was responsible for the homicide, perhaps even that you were engaged in self-defense and had no choice but to kill the victim. Cutting a body in order to dispose of it undetected is the most extreme form of defensive action. Forensic studies have shown that the few who engage in dismemberment have sometimes had exposure to hands-on anatomical dissection—as biology students, for example, or as hunters.

While cutting for reasons of sadism or pleasure is obviously an irrational act, criminal profilers say defensive dismemberment does not mean the killer is crazy, or a monster, as most people would suggest. Yet they also acknowledge that "something else is going on" inside the killer who has the capacity to do it. And no criminal profile has been developed for those who do.

# CHAPTER 12 ~ No Ordinary Fire

As Peter Abi-Rashed drove downtown on the morning of Saturday, April 10, he was buoyed by Ident's find in the basement, but also wary of what it could all mean for the investigation. How many of the body parts were in fact in the cooler and boxes? Could they prove the parts belonged to a murder victim? Did they all belong to one person? What could they prove about Sam Pirrera's role in the possible murder and dismemberment?

Abi-Rashed arrived at the hospital morgue at 10:19 a.m., where he met Ross Wood, who photographed the untouched seal on the cooler door. The detectives broke the seal, and that act, too, was photographed; every step documented, no holes in the case, no opening for a defense lawyer to pick at. Abi-Rashed opened the cooler door with his key; the gurney wheeled into the autopsy suite.

They grabbed a coffee a couple of doors down. At least the coffee shop was close, although next door to a morgue wasn't the best spot for one, certainly, Abi-Rashed reflected. You get a floater (remains that have decomposed) brought in for autopsy, the odor is overpowering, even down the hall, and you're in the coffee shop and you think, "On second thought, never mind."

The detectives joined others sitting on chairs around the examination table in the autopsy suite, including Ident man Curt Napholc, and a veteran detective named Mike Holk who was also assisting with the investigation. Dr. Chitra Rao, the forensic pathologist, began. In the early hours of the investigation, she had examined the pieces of human tissue found in Sam Pirrera's garbage. This time she had much more to study.

Napholc took a picture of the first box. Then a picture of the box being opened. Then with the box flaps open.

Remove one of the wrapped packages, photograph it. Unwrap. Photograph. Tag it. Photograph. Ross Wood, meanwhile, recorded each exhibit in his notebook. Each body part was wrapped in layers—plastic, shopping bags, towels. Each part took about 20 to 30 minutes to unwrap, record, and examine. The killer had likely used plastic wrappings in an attempt to conceal decomposition odor if the remains had to be left in storage for a long period of time, although this clearly had not been the case. The dismemberment had been very recent and so there was no human odor, only the smell of gasoline from the wrappings.

There were also bits of garbage, debris, inside each of the wrappings, which extended the examination time for each body part, as each piece of debris had to be removed, photographed, logged: torn cigaret package, cigaret butts, foil, plastic zip-lock baggies, earring, candle, copper crack pipe. The killer had been clinical in dismembering the body. Why the debris? He may have simply wanted to get rid of the debris from the crime scene, thinking it might offer police potential evidence if found.

One of the Ident detectives lifted a package from the cooler, unwrapped the layers. It was a knife, a long-handled butcher's knife, the kind you would find in anyone's kitchen. It was photographed, tagged. This was the tool used for the dismemberment. It had to be; it accounted for the clean cuts to the body parts and tissues.

Dr. Rao had worked as a forensic pathologist at the General full time since 1984, and presided over more than 200 homicide autopsies. Just one of those cases had been a dismemberment. The purpose of the autopsy is the same whether the body is dismembered or whole: the forensic pathologist tries to determine the cause of death, looking to the expired body to tell a story. But one complicating challenge in a dismemberment is determining whether all the parts in fact belong to the same body. She examined the parts one by one, placed each on the table in the correct anatomical position, as though rebuilding the victim. Right femur bone. Left femur bone. Right femur distal margin.

A package was unwrapped that contained the left lower arm and hand, severed at the elbow. Ident needed to roll a finger for a print, and compare it to missing persons recently called in to police. There was one female in particular that might provide a match: she had a criminal record and therefore had prints on file. In the autopsy suite, Ross Wood realized the missing woman's 10-print card—her fingerprint record—had been left back at the forensic services department at Central Station. Wood phoned the department and spoke to Ident detective Tim O'Keefe.

"We need her 10-print card," Wood said. "And some coffee."

O'Keefe arrived at the morgue, took the unknown victim's severed arm in his hands, grasped the left index finger, rolled the digit in black ink, and then pressed it to a card.

* * *

The autopsy stretched into the next day, Sunday, and part of Monday. By the conclusion, all the parts had been unwrapped and placed in correct anatomical position on the examination table. An entire body was accounted for, with the exception of some muscle tissue from the legs. It had been a complete dismemberment—assuming all of the parts belonged to the same victim, as it now appeared. A complete dismemberment, if done when the victim has just died, pre-rigor-mortis, with the right tools, can be accomplished in one to two hours. The one who did it had not been rushed, or sloppy; it was no hack job, but clinical, methodical. He had cut through the joints, not the bone, sliced away organs and muscle and viscera.

Forensic pathologist Dr. Chitra Rao.

Later, Dr. Chitra Rao and Peter Abi-Rashed chatted outside the autopsy suite—the doctor and the detective, two experts in homicide. Abi-Rashed was as tough as they came, figured he had seen it all, and Chitra Rao did not allow herself to be horrified by the things she saw in her morgue. About the only cases that would get to her were those involving children. She was not wired to venture into psychoanalysis, either. It was not her area of expertise. But this was one case that gave both of them pause on several levels.

"What makes a person do this?" she said. "You wonder if he had any feeling."

"You think you've seen everything," Abi-Rashed said. "And now this—you wonder how a human being could do it, take the time and deliberation."

It was a sentiment shared by all of the detectives working the case. Murder, they knew. People kill for money and love, out of anger gone haywire, a crazed mind. But the cold nature of the dismemberment, it was beyond the pale. That fact, the inhumanity of it all, accounted for their horror, made it the worst case they had ever seen. Later, in the Ident department, a few of the detectives viewed the photos from the autopsy, the severed parts, head, torso, limbs. There were grizzled veterans of bloody crime scenes, detectives who had up-close exposure to murder, to dismembered bodies from train track suicides, bloated corpses reeking of death found in the heat of summer. And still they could not believe it, could not believe someone could have butchered a human like this. The killer was one sick son of a bitch.

And yet, while unfathomable, you still have to rationalize a crime, understand what took place, and why, to try and crack the mystery. Peter Abi-Rashed and Chitra Rao talked about it.

"Why was the dismemberment done this way? What type of skills might a person need to do this? What trade might a person have, what interests?"

They talked about some of the points in the case so far. Among the items Ident had found in the rec room in Sam Pirrera's house were a bearskin and a wolf hide. He had hunting in his background. Clearly the dismemberment had been calculated, everything done for a reason, the manner of cutting, the wrapping, the storage. And the gasoline? Why were the wrapped parts in the basement dipped in accelerant? For setting them on fire, surely. But it would take prolonged, intense heat to do the job, to eliminate bone. No ordinary fire.

Gary Yokoyama

Sam's workplace, Dofasco.

If Sam Pirrera was responsible, his recent behavior at work, just prior to his arrest, revealed in documents seized by detectives at his workplace through search warrants, offered an explanation. On Monday, March 29, five days before the body parts were discovered outside his house, Sam reported to work at Dofasco. But that day he also visited the company's first aid department. He told an official there he was upset, so upset that he "did not feel safe at work." First aid sent him home. Four days after that, on Good Friday, the day before his arrest at the hospital, Sam returned to Dofasco even though he was not scheduled to report; he was still classified as being on stress leave. But Sam persisted, attempted to obtain medical clearance on the spot to get in to work. It was a holiday, the steel company had no one on staff available to give him that clearance. Sam pressed the issue further, someone made a phone call to a medical staffer, but clearance was still denied. He went back to his home. And it was the next day that his estranged wife Danielle found him in his house, curled in the fetal position on the couch, shaking.

Sam had been denied access to where he worked at Dofasco, in the melt shop. The melt shop, where scrap metal is superheated into liquid steel at temperatures as high as 1,700 degrees Celsius. That kind of heat would make almost anything vanish.

* * *

Dr. Chitra Rao noted in her post-mortem report that upon examining the victim's head, which was severed from the rest of the body, impressions on the skull were evident. They were "tramline" marks, parallel lines, suggesting blows from a thin cylindrical object. When you press down on your own skin with a finger, it temporarily leaves a mark, and a white blotch in the middle from where the blood diverted. A blow from a baseball bat, or stick, leaves a mark with a similar shape. A hammer, for example, would leave an entirely different impression. There were multiple marks on the skull from repeated blows. There were also teeth missing from the mouth.

The cause of death, she determined, was repeated blunt force trauma to the head. And the weapon?

The tramline markings on the skull were very narrow. Far too narrow for a baseball bat. One of the items removed from the cooler in the autopsy suite had been wrapped in a white towel, and also dipped in gasoline. Inside the towel was a pair of red and blue sport socks. And there was something else. A pool cue. A broken one.

Abi-Rashed could now see the attack in his mind's eye. It was swift and savage. Death came quickly. In the basement, the victim struck with the pool cue to the head; victim falls to the ground. There is little or no blood castoff spatter from the initial blow, but the continued beating on the floor mists blood on the lower wall from the force of impact; the dismemberment follows, probably right there in the basement, where there is enough space to do it; later, someone tries to clean away blood with disinfectant.

And the victim's identity?

Dr. Rao took DNA samples from every single part of the body for submission to the Centre of Forensic Sciences in Toronto. It would take time for the results to come back, to confirm for the record that all the parts belonged to the same person. She also sent tissue and blood samples to CFS for a toxicology test. The tox results revealed there was cocaine in the victim's bloodstream.

But before the CFS results could come back, right in the morgue, they could try and match fingerprints to establish identity on the spot. Prints are checked by comparing a series of points. Start, say, at the right delta. Go up five ridges, see what you find—a ridge ending? What about the other print? Go to another location, find a bifurcation. Does it match? Down the hall from the morgue in a separate office, Ident detective Tim O'Keefe had compared the print he had rolled from the victim's left index with one on file. Looked like he had his answer. A second Ident investigator must always go through the same process by choosing his own series of points for comparison. See if two sets of trained eyes come to the same conclusion. Ross Wood examined the prints. He agreed with O'Keefe. It was a match. They knew the name of the person murdered in Sam Pirrera's basement.

# CHAPTER 13 ~ HOLLOW STARE

When she was a teenager in the early 1980s, Maggie Karer left home, ran with the wrong crowd, got into drugs, which continued in her life in the lower city as an adult. In 1988, when Maggie was 23, she had a baby boy. She lived common law with the father, but it didn't last. She sometimes bumped into childhood friends like Kim Mcgilvery and Maria Barone. They were struck by how much she had changed physically, the hair no longer shiny, the complexion no longer radiant. It was the crack cocaine. Maria caught up with Maggie on the phone one day, talked about old times, lamented challenges in their lives. Maggie adored her son, but crack was dominating her life, she had started hooking to bankroll the addiction.

"At least you've had a good life," Maggie said.

"What happened to you, Maggie?" Maria asked.

"I have to support myself. I do what I have to do."

Maria felt it was like Maggie had lost any sense of herself; she no longer had faith in anything. The only thing she lived for was her son. She also didn't seem to have any role models to turn to, while at the same time possessing a devil-may-care spirit that made it difficult for anyone to reign her in. Perhaps her late father, big Les Karer, was the only one who could have.

In 1995 Maggie and her young son moved into a house on Maplewood in the lower city, near Gage Park. Her neighbor was Becky, the woman who would one day befriend Danielle Pirrera. Maggie was now 30, and, while crack had robbed her of some of the beauty of her youth, she was still an attractive woman, very slim, dark hair. Maggie rented the main level and basement of a duplex next door to Becky; Becky's son played with Maggie's boy. After a while there was a lot of activity at Maggie's during the day and night. Some nights, Becky would sit on the porch with her husband as fancy cars would come and go, entirely out of context with the neighborhood. Men were pulling up on the blue collar street in Mercedes Benzes, emerging from their cars wearing nice suits. Maggie had some high-powered clientele. It got so busy that men would come to her door, and Becky would ask, "You looking for Maggie? Next door."

Before long, the men visiting started to look rougher and rougher. One night, a guy was pounding on Maggie's door, yelling for her, accusing her of ripping him off. Maggie seemed the type who could handle herself fine. But every woman who works the street falls prey to crack and is abused at some point. It is part of the life.

Maggie's older brother invited her over for dinner, urged her to give up the drugs. Straighten your life out; it's not too late, he told her.

"I will. I will," she said.

Through it all she tried to be a good mother within the context of her life. Police patrolling downtown who knew Maggie, heard how dearly she loved her son. But crack continued to change her: the once pretty face showing the hollow stare of the crack addict, her movements becoming jerky. It all seemed to come in the space of less than a year. Her old friend Kim saw her once, on the street, working. Kim had long ago quit high school to get away from drugs, turned her life around. Maggie tried to avoid Kim when she spotted her.

"Kim, don't see me this way," she pleaded.

In 1998, Maggie put her name on a waiting list for a detox center. Was she just going through the motions? An addict will do anything, say anything, so long as they continue to have access to crack. There would have been a long road ahead to kick the addiction that had taken control of her life, but her family and friends felt it was a sign that, finally, she had decided to clean herself up for her son, and herself. Kim heard that Maggie's name was on a waiting list. She wondered if Maggie's life might have turned out differently if she'd got help right away.

Easter weekend 1999 approached. Maggie made plans to have Easter dinner with her mother and brother. On Wednesday morning, March 31, at about 4 a.m., Maggie Karer stood at a pay phone at the corner of Main and Melrose downtown. It was close to the Montrose Apartments, where the father of Maggie's son stayed. The father was known as Bugsy. A dealer lived there, too, and girls like Maggie would hit the street, hook, bring money back to the dealer who would then give them crack to smoke, and a room. The girls would sometimes be up for four, five days at a time, hooking, using, over and over, until exhausted. Maggie had bottomed out; she was using so much that, like any addict, she was playing catch-up, smoking crack trying to normalize her emotions—without success.

A taxi pulled up next to the pay phone where Maggie stood. The cabbie, Bryan, had known Maggie for about a year, and he too lived at the Montrose. He had first met her when she flagged him down outside a hotel downtown. Maggie was dressed nicely that night, looked like she was escorting, although she didn't have her six dollar fare with her. She probably did have the cash but was hoarding it for crack. Bryan let it go. They became friends and he became a dependable ride. The girls were paranoid about undercover police; the vice cops sometimes posed as cabbies. Maggie and Bryan used together. She also ripped him off for a couple of hundred bucks on a drug deal once. Bryan was OK with it. He tried to kick the addiction, but it wasn't easy in that apartment building. Maggie and another girl would come to his door late at night.

"So Bryan, you being good tonight, or bad?"

At the pay phone, Maggie wore faded jeans, a tank top, and a jacket made of some kind of leather or suede. She was a bit older than the other girls, had become painfully thin, her cheeks sunken. Maggie held the phone, gave the cabbie the look, and the grin. *You want something?* She asked if he wanted to use with her.

"I'm clean, Maggie," Bryan said. "Went to treatment in December. If you ever get tired of the misery, there's a way out."

She turned and started talking on the phone.

Sometime between that Wednesday morning, and Good Friday, April 2, Sam Pirrera, in the midst of a week-long crack binge, and attending Narcotics Anonymous meetings with his sponsor, picked up Maggie Karer and took her to his home. It was not the first time she had been to Sam's house to use. But this time, it did not go smoothly. She wanted to leave.

*"You're not going anywhere."*

# CHAPTER 14 ~ UNDERGROUND TRIBUTE

Every day during the investigation, Peter Abi-Rashed had written notes in his white homicide casebook, the one labeled "J. Doe." And now the case had a name. Karer. The fingerprints rolled in the Hamilton General Hospital morgue belonged to Margaret (Maggie) Karer. Date of birth: Sept. 22, 1964. Date of death: likely within three days of the discovery of the body parts on April 3, 1999.

Maggie, Daddy's little girl with the golden brown hair; teenager at Hill Park high school; young woman on the vacation of her life in Hungary; mother to a young son. A life on the edge in the lower city; prostitution, crack. Murdered and carved to pieces in Sam Pirrera's basement.

At some point after he had not heard from her for a few days, Maggie's older brother had a dream one night. He dreamt he was home and heard knocking on the front door. Who was there? In the dream, he did not answer the door, even as he had a sense that it was Maggie knocking. As headlines splashed across *The Hamilton Spectator* about body parts found at the home of Sam Pirrera—a name Maggie's brother had never heard before—he tried not to think the worst. But still. Maggie lived a life that could bring her in contact with very bad people.

On Saturday night, April 10, he heard a knock for real at this door. He answered. It was a police officer. "I've got some news I have to tell you," the officer said. Right away, Maggie's brother knew. The officer drove him in the cruiser up the Mountain where they met with Margaret Karer, Maggie's mother, and broke the news to her. Maggie was dead. She broke down, her world completely shattered.

"No! Maggie, my Maggie!" she shouted, weeping. "That—creature, that monster, has done this to my princess, my Maggie."

Maggie Karer's police mug shot.

Hamilton Police released the victim's name to the media; those who had reported loved ones feared missing needed to know the body had been identified as Maggie Karer. Her old high school friends, Kim and Maria, were shocked when they saw the police mug shot of Maggie splashed across the front page of *The Hamilton Spectator*. It was an image so far removed from the pretty girl they knew growing up. Her life as a prostitute was repeatedly mentioned in the media. The *Toronto Sun* tabloid referred to her as a "Hamilton hooker." It was though that was her title, her essence, and Maggie's family and old friends were appalled by the coverage. The sum of her life was more than that.

Late in the afternoon of Tuesday, April 13, with security tight, Sam Pirrera entered a Hamilton courtroom dressed

in orange prisoner coveralls, shackled at the hands and feet. Standing before Justice of the Peace Cathy Woron, he was remanded in custody until April 21. He said nothing in court.

Maggie Karer's remains were cremated, the funeral held Saturday, April 24, at St. Stephen of Hungary Roman Catholic Church on Barton Street East. Maggie's mother and brother were there, aunts and uncles, a couple of old friends, and her son, who

Sam Pirrera in shackles.

was 10 years old. It was a small ceremony. The family did not want media there; they were still bitter over the coverage.

Everyone could feel Sam Pirrera's shadow at the funeral. And he was, in fact, nearly right across the street from the church, in the Barton Street jail, awaiting his next court date. Some felt anger, leaving the church, seeing the place where Maggie's murderer continued to live. Her ashes were buried at Holy Sepulchre Cemetery in Burlington, a photo laid in the stone of Maggie as a teenager—the bright smile, radiant skin, eyes alive.

Friends Kim (left) and Maria were badly shaken.

Kim and Maria were badly shaken. Right after the news of the murder broke, the two friends drove up to the house on Burns Place together, brought flowers and poems, which they laid at the base of a large tree in the front yard. For several days after that, they drove up there, parking near the house, just talking, as though the yard was Maggie's gravesite. Nightmares violated Maria's sleep; she could see Maggie being beaten, dismembered. She fell into depression.

Kim organized a memorial at Gage Park for friends who had not been at the church. She held it near the swing set.

Kim thought that was the perfect place, near children. That's how she wanted to remember Maggie, as a child. Kim read the Lord's Prayer and everyone joined in. There were about 15 people, mostly women, no family. Kim had a speech prepared, but when the time came, she just went from the heart. It felt right.

"People need to remember Maggie as a vibrant, carefree girl," she said. "A girl with chestnut hair and olive skin. She had a smile that could melt your heart. Do not judge Maggie. Do not judge what she did or who she became. Judge her by who she was: a caring, loving mother who loved her son, loved her parents."

A couple of Hamilton plainclothes police officers were there, lingering back from the gathering, checking to see who might show at the service, potential friends of Maggie's they could interview. When the police left, several other people appeared who had been watching from a distance. Now they gathered around Kim. They were women who worked the streets. They thanked Kim for having the event. One broke down crying, said she wanted to get herself clean, get out of the life. Kim and a friend tried to help her. Two months later, that same woman was back on the streets. Maggie's photo from the newspaper, meanwhile, was taped up in crack houses in Hamilton as a kind of underground tribute.

Photo courtesy of the author

The Maggie her old friends remembered.

There was one woman who worked the streets who felt an unusual connection to Maggie. Her name was Lynn Murray. Sometime in the weeks before Maggie was murdered, Sam had hit on Lynn at a Narcotics Anonymous meeting downtown. Lynn's street names at the time were Brenda or Tracy. She worked for an escort service, where she had become addicted to crack. It felt like a good thing at first. The drug made her feel euphoric, helped numb her to the job and the sick things she did for clients. She was 23 years old, five-foot-two, 100 pounds, long hair that she alternated between blond and red. At a break in a meeting at the church, a group of them stood outside smoking. That's when Sam approached her. "I'm picking up," he said. "Do you want to come back to my place and party?"

Lynn's instincts were immediate upon hearing the question. "Picking up" meant he was getting crack. There would be a chance to use, although sex would also be part of it. Yes, she would love to do the crack, she needed it. She had seen Sam at meetings before—he had sat beside her—but she never found him at all attractive. But tonight he was picking up, and that was enough for her.

Before she could accept his offer, a friend pulled her aside. It was Bryan, who drove a cab, who knew Maggie. He urged Lynn not to go, not because he had anything against Sam, who he did not know, but because he knew it was usually a bad thing for women to hook up with men at the meetings. Guys sometimes preyed on women there, when they were at their most vulnerable. Lynn did not go with Sam Pirrera that night. Later, when she heard about Maggie, she felt sad for her, but she also felt profound relief. Maggie might have taken her place, she felt.

Another woman who paid close attention to the news

*The Hamilton Spectator*

Tears at the memorial for Maggie Kare.

of Maggie Karer's murder was the woman with the deep tan and blond hair named Jean. She saw the pictures of the house on Burns Place in the newspaper and read that Sam Pirrera had been charged with the murder. *Sam*? Jean had been the one Sam hit on at the AA meeting, she had been right there, in Sam's house, in his hot tub, and basement, a little more than a week before Maggie's murder.

She thought back to her experience, terrified all over again. That night at 12 Burns Place, Jean had told Sam she wanted to leave, and he had reacted angrily. As they sat on the couch watching TV, she tried again, offered to call a cab herself to get home.

"No, I'll drive you," Sam snapped back angrily.

When Sam and Jean got into his white Cougar, he did not hold the door for her the way he had when he first picked her up on the date. He just got in his driver's side and slammed the door hard. He was silent the five minutes on the drive back to Jean's place. He said nothing until she got out of the car.

"I'll call you," Sam finally said. Jean said nothing, knew she never wanted to see him again. His anger and dark aura had frightened her. The next day, Jean phoned her AA sponsor, explained her fears.

"If your gut is telling you that, then don't go back to him," the sponsor said. "Use me as your excuse; tell him that I said you're not allowed to date anyone from the meetings."

The very next afternoon, Jean saw the white Cougar pull into her driveway. He hadn't called first, just showed up. Oh my God, she thought. She was alone, her kids were still with her estranged husband. She let him in, poured him a cup of tea—except that with her nerves on edge, she accidentally mixed chocolate milk into the tea. She thought her mistake was kind of funny, actually, but Sam got ticked off, glowered at her. He was there for about 45 minutes. Jean didn't say much, and he left. She never heard from Sam Pirrera again.

And now this. Murder. The victim, Maggie Karer—it could have been me, Jean thought. She felt relief. And guilt. She wondered if she'd been the one that pushed Sam over the edge, so that the next woman who came to his house suffered. Why didn't he attack her? Was it because he was not using crack or booze that night? Is that what saved her? Years later, Jean told her teenage daughters the story. Never do what she did: never go to a strange man's house alone like that, she told them.

After hearing the news, Jean called the police and went down to Central Station and was interviewed by a detective. She figured they could use her information. And she also came forward, she told the detective, because she figured her fingerprints were all over Sam's house and they'd probably find her eventually and want to learn what she knew.

"Well, have you ever been fingerprinted before?" the detective asked her.

"No."

"Then we wouldn't have ever known who you were."

Jean felt a chill. If she had been murdered in that house, and her body disposed of, maybe no one would ever have known what happened to her; she told no one that she had gone to Sam Pirrera's house that night, a man she had never met before.

She rose to leave the police station. Jean had not always had an easy life, but always had a sense that God was keeping her alive for a reason, usually small things, like if her car broke down it happened in a good place. And it had happened again.

"If I were you, I'd buy a lottery ticket on the way home," the detective said.

# CHAPTER 15 ~ CYCLE OF ABUSE

Peter Abi-Rashed knew the case his team was building against Sam Pirrera in the murder of Maggie Karer was strong. Under questioning Sam had admitted having a woman in his house near the time Maggie was murdered. His estranged wife Danielle had told police that Sam admitted that he killed a hooker and dismembered her body. Danielle had also told police that she noticed clear plastic lining in the trunk of Sam's car in the days prior to the discovery of the body parts. The Centre of Forensic Sciences in Toronto confirmed that all of the parts examined at the autopsy in fact belonged to Maggie.

Sam's house had been revealed as the scene of the murder and dismemberment. They had the suspected murder weapon, the broken pool cue hidden in the fruit cellar, the cause of death a blunt force to the head. They had the knife used for the dismemberment. The weapon, the knife, and body parts had been soaked in gasoline for disposal. And Sam had tried desperately to get in to work at Dofasco on Good Friday, when he was not scheduled to do so—which was right around the time Maggie was murdered. He worked in the melt shop, where the body parts, and other evidence, could have been incinerated. During interrogation, Sam had offered no defense other than accusing Danielle of lying, and claiming that the woman who visited his home had left safely by taxi. Detectives investigated with city taxi services and found no evidence of any cabs going to Burns Place in the days before the body parts were found.

And still, at the end of April the search of Sam's house continued. Ident detectives Ross Wood, Gary Zwicker, and Curt Napholc took the place apart, taking no chance of missing evidence of another victim—body parts, videotapes, other previously undetected signs of foul play—or evidence that could reconstruct more precisely what had happened to Maggie in that house. Ident was still combing through the house into May, six weeks from the time the first search warrant had been approved when the case broke.

It was a long haul for the detectives; they were working 14- to16-hour days. They started at Central Station early each morning, just after 7 a.m. with a briefing by Abi-Rashed, grabbed a coffee and headed up the Mountain to the house, where they worked till 9 or 10 p.m. It wasn't the first time Wood, the veteran of the team, had been away at a scene for a long stretch all hours of the day. His wife, Marjory, knew the drill. She even brought cookies to the Ident van at the scene for the guys. When it was all over, Wood came home and said, "Remember me?"

Ident took more than 2,000 photos in that house, and Zwicker snapped most of them. Zwicker, though he had served as a police officer for 12 years, was new to Ident and extended forensic searches. He had just met a woman named Cindy. Their first date was on March 31, right before he got locked down with the case. He couldn't make any plans as the search dragged on. Talk about getting off on the wrong foot. He sent her a card: "It won't always be like this!" As it happened, Cindy stuck with Zwick and eventually they got married.

Inside the house, the detectives turned off the lights in each room, closed blind, and sprayed luminol looking for blood. Luminol is a chemical that reacts with iron in hemoglobin. When blood is present, the spray turns a bright blue in the dark. Traces of blood glowed in the kitchen, a strong reaction on the floor. Could be a false positive; cleaning solutions react with luminol as well. But there were also blood reactions in the living room and by the rear porch. They sprayed in the fruit cellar where the body parts had been hidden. On a concrete wall the luminol revealed what looked like a bloody handprint. Someone had since scrubbed the wall with some kind of cleanser, making the print invisible to the naked eye. Who spent so much time cleaning the house? Sam Pirrera?

They figured blood would show on the dark red carpet near the pool table, the area where they suspected the murder had taken place. On their hands and knees, Wood, Napholc, and Zwicker felt dampness in the red carpet with the black swirl pattern. Luminol sprayed on the carpet. A reaction. Cleaner, certainly, but also, the detectives felt, definitely blood. A large volume of blood.

"It's lighting up like Las Vegas," Zwicker said.

More spray. A shape started to take form through the blue glow—the outline of a body. A picture of what probably happened in the house had come into focus. The broken front storm door, blood here and there on the main floor—a fight starting upstairs, continuing down in the basement. A vicious beating in the rec room, beside the pool table. And dismemberment of the body on the carpet. Finally, a vigorous cleanup.

Gary Yokoyama

Detective Dave Place.

The Karer case was solid. But Abi-Rashed was focusing more on expanding the net. What happened to Sam's first wife, Beverly? Through the spring, Major Crime Detective Dave Place continued trying to find her. Communication was Place's strength; he would eventually gain a reputation as one of the best interviewers in the police service. He just had that way about him—easygoing, honest, could get anyone to talk. He interviewed Bev's old friends and family. Where had she been the last eight years?

\* \* \*

Morning light poured through the bedroom window in the Davidson house on Adams Street. And when the young bride stared at the placid face of her new husband, Sam Pirrera, Bev's heart swelled with love.

Against the wishes of parents of both families, Sam and Bev wed on May 12, 1986. Sam had recently turned 19, Bev was just 16, three months from her 17th birthday. In one picture, the young couple looked small, as though it was a snapshot from a high school grad dance rather than a wedding. In the photo Sam wore a black jacket, shirt casually open at the neck, Bev in a simple white dress, wispy, light, and lacy; her hair blond, face rosy and fresh and young. Bev glowed in the photo but Sam had the downward, evasive cast in his eyes that had always bothered Lesa Davidson, Bev's mother.

The witness who signed Bev's portion of the marriage certificate was her father, Doug Davidson. The witness signing for Sam was a woman named Jeanne Partridge. His parents, Antonio and Lina Pirrera, did not attend the wedding. Some said that they were not even aware of the wedding, that Sam had kept it a secret because they were so opposed to him marrying Beverly Davidson. Others believed they knew of the wedding but chose to boycott it because they were so disillusioned with Sam's lifestyle, his drug abuse. Bev's mom always felt that they didn't attend because they disapproved of a non-Italian marrying into their family, and that they had never liked Bev. The two families did not get along from the beginning.

Sam and Bev couldn't afford their own place so they lived upstairs in the Davidson home, right down the hall from Bev's parents. Lesa Davidson could barely stand it. Sam did not treat Bev well, did not talk nicely to her, even in front of

Lesa. From the moment they started dating, Sam had never recognized boundaries of civility like that, was too cocky to consider being more discreet. Later in his life, some would say that his attitude towards girlfriends was simply a reflection of the hatred he felt for women in general.

Lesa had told Bev it was a bad situation. Sam was not right for her.

"But Mom, when he first wakes up in the morning, he looks gorgeous," she said.

"Then you must have your eyes closed because he doesn't look too good to me."

Sam had completed Grade 12 at Scott Park high school, where he was a B student. He worked for a few years as a cook at a Kentucky Fried Chicken. Then he worked for Automotive Parts and Performance as a dispatcher in shipping and receiving, making $5.75 an hour. He submitted a resumé to Dofasco, where his father, Antonio, worked, and was hired on to work casual shifts.

"I'd be very happy to work at Dofasco because of everything it has to offer," Sam wrote. "And I think it would be very good for my future." His father, and a friend, were listed as his references. Under "other activities," he wrote, "Working on cars and playing hockey"; under "Department Applying For," he put, "Oxygen steelmaking, No. 2 Melt Shop."

His relationship with Bev, meanwhile, had always been chaotic, and marriage did not smooth the waters. Sam had been possessive of her from the start, as though he feared any outside influence eroding his control over her. Not long after their wedding, they moved out of Bev's parents' house on Adams Street and got an apartment on nearby Wentworth Street. But he refused to let Bev go home to spend time with her mother. Bev even hesitated to sneak a visit when Sam was at work, in case she was spotted by Sam's family, who lived on Cannon Street across from Adams.

The heated arguments between Sam and Bev continued.

As had become Sam's pattern, he acted out physically when angry. Just a few weeks after their wedding Bev showed up at St. Joseph's Hospital with a black eye, a swollen face, bruising. Sam had punched her in the face, several times. She called police and he was charged with assault. They broke up, but were soon back together. The court sentence said Sam was to live at his parents' home on Cannon Street, advise police of any change of address, keep the peace, and "be of good behaviour particularly towards Beverly Pirrera."

Sam's criminal record continued to grow: speeding; failure to produce insurance; three more speeding tickets. In December 1986, he was convicted of narcotics possession. A month later, Bev became pregnant, and he was charged with assaulting her a second time. Bev said he had kicked her in the stomach. She kept returning to him, though, the cycle of abuse and reconciliation now central to their relationship.

Early in the marriage, Bev started working as an exotic dancer at Hanrahan's strip club on Barton Street East. Bev started picking up shifts dancing when she was 17 or 18 years old. It was Sam's idea—he had friends who worked at a few of the clubs. It was not work Bev was proud of, she would not even talk about it with friends. To the extent she did talk about it, Bev said she had to do it, Sam made her, because the extra money helped bankroll his drug tab. She could make $500 to $1,000 a week at Hanrahan's or area clubs like Debonair, Pandora's Box, and Johnny U's. She was the headline act at one of them.

Sam profited from her work, but at the same time it inflamed his jealousy. The paranoia common in crack users only made it worse. Didn't everyone have an eye for beautiful Bev? Hadn't they always? And there she was, for all to see—and was she looking back? He sat there in the club, cloaked in darkness but for shards of white from black light in the joint, staring not at the blond on stage, but instead surveying the crowd, the men at their tables watching the show in slack-jawed silence, ready to cast an evil eye at any man thinking of hitting on her. At the end of Bev's shift, he always drove her home from work immediately, never allowing her to chat with anyone.

They continued to fight, break up, get back together again. On August 6, 1987, with Bev a couple of weeks away from giving birth to their first child, and the couple temporarily split up, Sam was charged with making harassing phone calls to her—charges Bev later dropped. Late in August she gave birth to a girl five weeks premature. Bev named her Ashlee, her last name registered as Davidson.

Sam, Bev, and baby Ashlee.

In September, Sam was suspended from Dofasco for falling asleep on the job and being constantly late. He told his boss he was not getting enough sleep because of marital problems. "Apparently he recently argued with his wife ... threatened her and she charged him," wrote a Dofasco supervisor in an evaluation of Sam. "However, he claims he's not worried about this, she has charged him in the past and the charges are always dropped. He denies any alcohol or drug problem, and that what's really bothering him is not being settled with his wife, as well as 'interference' from both families. In spite of this, he feels he can handle the situation himself and does not want outside assistance."

Sam and Bev reconciled yet again, and moved with Ashlee into an apartment. On February 29, 1988, Hamilton police raided the apartment looking for drugs. Sam had long been on their radar for drug offences. And they found his stash: crack cocaine, some LSD. Meanwhile, Sam continued to abuse Bev, by her count he assaulted her on seven occasions. She withdrew charges five of those times. She moved out with Ashlee, seeking refuge for three days at Inasmuch House, a Hamilton women's shelter. Then she went back to her mother. But, ultimately, she was back with Sam once more.

# Chapter 16 ~ "Be Right Back, Mom"

Lesa Davidson urged her daughter to leave him for good. "Bev, if they beat you once, they are always going to beat you," she said.

How did he always manage to get her back? Sam had some kind of psychological hold on Bev, Lesa thought. One day, Sam sat in the Davidson home. Bev had visible bruising on her face. She left the room, and Lesa turned to Sam.

"You did that to her," she said.

Sam just looked at Lesa, said nothing, and smiled. She burned.

"If I find out you did that to her, you'll deal with me," she said in her French-Canadian accent. "She'll stay with me."

"No," Sam finally replied. "Nobody else will ever have her."

Bev had a feisty, independent streak, but she could not break out of the cycle, and their shared child complicated matters. When they had first met, she listened to Sam, his stories about growing up, the personal issues with his own family he poured out to her. Did she feel a bond with him, despite it all? Did she feel sorry for him, searching for a vulnerability in the man beneath the often monstrous exterior?

Perhaps it was simply the smallness of Beverly Davidson's world; each time she tried to leave Sam, she never got farther than her mom down the street, or a shelter downtown, never really venturing beyond Hamilton's weathered northeast end. Her parents had never graduated from high school, she had a younger brother, but no older sibling to turn to for advice. Her parents' marriage had fallen apart. Lesa and Doug Davidson divorced not long after Bev and Sam wed. Bev had met Sam when she was barely 15; she could never get beyond the walls established by Sam, and by her own circumstances.

On August 9, 1988, Bev tried to break off with him but this time he put both his hands around her neck and started strangling her. Bev, who was five-foot-six, about 110 pounds, felt herself passing out before he let go. Don't charge me, please, he later begged. And Bev agreed, if he vowed never to come near her again.

Bev lived in an apartment on Wentworth Street with a friend, then returned to Adams Street, where her mother could help care for her little girl. Sam's shadow still loomed, as usual, from where he again lived with his parents on Cannon. On September 9, Bev sat in a bar called the Jockey Club, in Dorsey's Lounge. It was just after 8 p.m., and she looked across the room and saw Sam sitting at the bar. He made an obscene gesture at her. She went to the bouncer, a man she knew, and complained about it. The bouncer walked over to Sam.

"Are we going to have any trouble here?" he said. Bev left. Sam fumed.

Another night Sam followed Bev home from a bar, drove his car slowly alongside her. She reported the incidents to the police as stalking. In an effort to perhaps beat Bev to the punch, and to win custody of Ashlee, Sam filed divorce papers. The filing began an exchange of court documents between the couple. He based the divorce petition on the claim that Bev had committed adultery. He alleged his wife had slept with a neighbor while he was working the night shift at Dofasco. On October 14, 1988, he signed an affidavit requesting custody, accusing Bev of being an "unsettled" person, who had "a history of exotic dancing" and had attempted suicide in the past. Bev replied on November 14, citing Sam's well-documented physical abuse and cocaine addiction. As for the suicide attempt, she admitted to overdosing on pills in 1986.

"The reason was a reaction to the extreme beatings that I was receiving from my husband," she wrote. Bev added that she was forced to dance to "support his cocaine habit."

And she alleged that Sam's mother, Lina Pirrera, had pushed her down the stairs when she was 12 weeks pregnant. Sam's mother responded in an affidavit, denying ever pushing Bev down the stairs.

Sam returned fire, denying "each and every allegation." He said he had kicked his coke habit, and accused Bev of harassing him, attacking him "when she didn't get her way," and cutting him in the chest with a knife. Bev danced for her own benefit, because of her "jealousy about not having the things other people had."

On March 3, 1989, a court order was made granting interim care of Ashlee to Bev's mother as the custody battle between Sam and Bev continued. A social worker was assigned to evaluate who was best suited to care for the baby. The social worker interviewed Sam, Bev, and parents on both sides. She filed a report on July 12, 1989:

"My impression of this couple's relationship can be summed up in one word: chaotic. Bev states that Sam was very heavily into drugs and beat her up on several occasions. Sam states that he was heavily into drugs but beat up Bev on only one occasion after she took a knife to him...The families of Sam and Bev do not get along, in fact, there is open hostility."

The report portrayed both Sam and Bev as having made mistakes in the relationship, but sided overall with Sam: "Sam states he has been free of his drug habit since March 1988." It quoted a Dofasco official who said Sam was a reliable and conscientious employee. On the other hand, Bev, wrote the social worker, has an "extremely unsettled" lifestyle. "The situation as it now exists is one that is full of hostility—especially on the part of Bev and her mother against Sam. Sam appears almost naïve about this and avoids confrontations...Bev seems determined to 'win' no matter what it takes, i.e. hiring a private investigator to follow Sam." Bev needs time to "mature and organize her own life" before she can look after her daughter, the report concluded. And while "there is no doubt Sam has tried hard to make a good impression throughout this assessment" he comes across as a caring father.

The social worker recommended that Sam be granted interim custody of their daughter: "The security, stability, stimulation, structure, family life and values must all be considered. In the long term, it seems that Sam and his family can best meet those requirements. Despite the drug involvement and all the problems because of it, there is a solid core to Sam's personality. The gentleness, concern, and listening ability that attracted Bev to him are features of that personality that continue to be evident."

*A solid core to Sam's personality.*

Two months later, on September 21, Sam was convicted on three counts of possession of narcotics, fined $500 on each of two counts, and received one month in jail on another. Two months after that he was charged for not wearing a seatbelt. Then a charge for speeding. A month later, drunk driving.

Even after all the affidavits, charges, and countercharges, Sam and Bev got back together once again, their shared daughter their one remaining bond. In January 1990, the three of them moved into a two-bedroom unit in a 58-unit subsidized social housing townhouse complex at Barton Street and Kenora Avenue. They had regained joint custody of Ashlee—and Bev was pregnant a second time with Sam's child. The baby was born in September 1990. It was a boy, named Matthew. In January 1991, the family moved to a larger unit with three bedrooms in the same complex.

By the spring of 1991, the reconciliation was again on the rocks. Bev, who was now 21, believed she could leave Sam once and for all. In May, Bev was at her mom's house on Adams Street. Her fifth wedding anniversary with Sam was a week away. She told her mom about her intentions to finally leave him. Lesa Davidson was relieved.

The phone rang. Lesa answered. It was Sam. He wanted to speak to Bev. He said he would come by to pick her up. Bev told her mother that she and Sam needed to return briefly to the townhouse, she had to retrieve some things she had left there, some clothes. Sam drove over to Adams Street in the metallic grey 1973 Cutlass that Bev's dad had sold to him. He pulled up in an alley behind the Davidson house and, as usual, did not come inside. Just as when they were teens, he waited for Bev to come to him, avoiding her mother.

Bev was dressed in shorts and T-shirt, her hair tied back in a ponytail. She walked out the door, no jacket, no purse. Lesa could see Sam in the driver's seat; she made brief eye contact with him. He looked directly at her. Sam did not smile.

"Be right back, Mom," Bev called as she walked away from the house. And she was gone.

Three days passed, and Bev still had not come home. Lesa Davidson noticed Sam moving belongings into his parents' house across the street on Cannon. Lesa phoned him.

"Where is Bev?" she asked.

"She left—someone picked her up," Sam said. "She said to tell you she'll be in touch."

Sam and Bev's townhouse complex.

* * *

In the summer of 1991, Sam Pirrera filed court papers looking to divorce Bev and gain full custody of their two young
children. "There is no possibility of reconciliation between the
respondent and myself," said the claim. "The present situation
is that the respondent has again gone back to exotic dancing
and possibly prostitution."

Sam had accused Bev of many things in his previous sworn
affidavits. This was the first time he had gone so low as to suggest his wife now worked the street. Bev had always answered
Sam's accusations with affidavits of her own. This was the first
time in their legal battle she did not file a response.

He claimed they had separated May 17, 1991 and "since
that time there has been no cohabitation." He added that Bev's
current address was her mother's house on Adams Street.
In another document he said Bev had telephoned and said
she was in California, "although I have no way of knowing
if this is true."

At the end of May, he had told the company running the
subsidized townhouse complex where he and Bev lived that he
was moving out on short notice. "My wife left me two weeks
ago," he said. "She took the two kids. I'd like to leave by the
end of June; I'm moving in with my parents."

Later in the summer, he filed an affidavit saying he was
caring for the two kids at his parents' house and Bev "has
showed no interest in the children and in fact has not even
made an attempt to see them for one month…The respondent
is not capable of looking after the children because of her
lifestyle at the present time. She is a very selfish individual
who thinks only of her own interests." Bev may be "going
back and forth" to the United States and might "try to take
the children."

Once again there was no response from Bev.

On July 3, Sam served an official application for divorce. Bev did not reply.

"The only place where I can think of where the respondent would go," Sam said, "would be her mother's place.... I do not believe advertising in the newspaper in the area would do any good because I do not believe she is still in the area. In fact, she is an exotic dancer. I do not know where she is working at the present time."

At the end of July 1991, a court order was issued directing Bev to respond to Sam's motions. Again she did not respond. That summer, the phone rang in the Davidson home on Adams Street. Lesa Davidson was not home; she worked a night shift. Lori, her daughter-in-law, answered.

"Hello?"

"It's Bev. Mom there?"

"She's at work."

"Tell her I'm in California. I'm doing OK, I'll call her later."

It was an odd phone call. To Lori the voice didn't even sound much like Bev's. And strange that she didn't seem anxious to talk with her when she'd been away. There were two other similarly brief phone calls in the space of three months. Looking for answers, Lesa asked Sam about it. Why wasn't she calling home more, or visiting? Bev had confided in her in the past; why not now? Maybe she had changed, or maybe Bev just wanted to keep away from Sam and have no contact with anyone back in Hamilton.

"She knows you're going to be upset with her," Sam told Lesa. "I'm sure she'll call you when she's ready."

Lesa Davidson, meanwhile, wanted to see her grandchildren and phoned Sam to tell him so. One day he dropped by the Davidson house with Ashlee and Matthew. Sam talked about Bev being in California. He had talked to her recently, he said. Bev was doing well. She had told him that she recently mailed birthday presents to give to the kids.

Lesa had been surprised and hurt that Bev had left her kids and family like that, and gone so far away without even saying goodbye. But at least it sounded like she was OK.

The next summer, on August 20, 1992, Sam and Bev's divorce was finalized. It was signed on October 29. The court declared that Sam be awarded full custody of both kids: "Beverly Ann Davidson shall have no access to the said children until further order of the court." Bev, who had not filed a single response to the court since Sam had initiated the divorce petition, was also ordered to pay $100 a month in child support, and costs.

Sam brought the kids over to visit Lesa Davidson again. She dearly missed seeing them regularly. Inside the house on Adams Street, Ashlee, who was five, paused in front of a photo of a girl hanging on the wall.

"Who's that?" the girl asked.

"That's Bev, that's your mommy," Lesa replied.

Ashlee started to ask more questions. "Where is my mommy?"

Lesa tried to answer the little girl as best she could. And Sam Pirrera stopped bringing the kids over to Nana's house.

# Chapter 17 ~ Darkest Secret

Detective Dave Place continued to search for Beverly Davidson through the spring of 1999, as Sam Pirrera awaited his next court date in the Maggie Karer homicide. It is difficult, though not impossible, for an individual to disappear on purpose. A key factor is whether you have the financial resources to vanish—leave the country, survive without needing to use credit cards, or social services that are traceable.

Place learned that Bev did not fall into that category. In her entire life she had never had much money to her name. But there are other trails people leave. Place searched provincial and national health records, driver's license records. Through the fraud branch, police searched financial records, credit card data, phone records, dental records. In interviews Place conducted with family members and friends who hadn't seen Bev in years, there was no suggestion she had ever talked of making any move from Hamilton.

Bev's old friend Karen had never understood what happened. Karen knew how miserable Bev had been with Sam. Might she have yearned to break free, start fresh as far away as possible? Karen knew one thing for sure: Bev would never willingly leave her kids. She was a doting mother. Since they didn't disappear along with her, something had to be amiss.

Hamilton Police Service

Dave Place went international in his search, working through the FBI, American state police forces, and Interpol. He looked for tips from law enforcement in California, the place where Sam had repeatedly claimed Bev had moved, about unidentified bodies that had been found. None of the reported cases had any similarities to Bev.

Bev vanished without a trace.

As the weeks wore on, Place still could find no record of Beverly's existence since the time in May 1991 when her mother had last seen her. According to Ontario driver's license data, her last recorded address as of February 21, 1991, was 2344 Barton St. E., Unit 38—the townhouse she had shared with Sam. Her driver's license expired on July 12, 1991 and was never renewed. Place learned that the only person who had reported a sighting of Bev, in fact, was Sam Pirrera. He had told several people that Bev had returned from California a few years back at Christmas time. He said Bev showed up at his house, wanted to see the two kids, but he turned her away. She had been a bad mother, run off, Sam said, so he wouldn't let her in the door.

But there was no evidence that Bev had been anywhere in Hamilton, or anywhere else, since May 1991. She was gone. Place was disappointed. Her disappearance without a trace elevated the case against Sam Pirrera, but Dave Place had started his search with the assumption that she was alive, somewhere, and that he would find her.

The detective met with Peter Abi-Rashed to update him on the case. Abi-Rashed listened. There was no absolute proof

Gary Yokoyama

Karen had no idea what happened to her friend Bev.

she was dead, but Abi-Rashed knew what it all meant. The circumstantial evidence was clear enough. Beverly Davidson by all accounts adores her two kids, and in fact fights Sam repeatedly for custody—and then just leaves the kids without saying a word? Tells none of her friends or family that she's taking off? Never calls—apart from mysterious calls by someone claiming to be Beverly? And the only evidence that she was still alive and had left town comes from Sam?

Abi-Rashed was certain that Bev had been murdered and her body disposed of. The clinical, methodical nature of the Karer dismemberment unveiled at the autopsy was burned in his mind's eye. Sam knew what he was doing, was convinced he would get away with it. Because he had done it before. The question was, could that be proven in court? They had no body and no crime scene. Could she have been killed by someone else? She worked in exotic dancing, lived in a rough part of town. If she had been murdered by Sam, it had happened perhaps eight years ago. They had only conjecture, and circumstantial evidence was tenuous. If Sam did it, he was probably the only witness. And Sam had admitted nothing. Or had he?

More information was about to come the detective's way, and it came indirectly courtesy of Pirrera himself, a product of his own pathologies, the combination of his ego and desire to control his women with fear. Once Bev was gone, he had badmouthed her to several people, but he had also talked about the end of his relationship with her. He had talked a little too much. One of those people he talked to about it, was his ex-wife Danielle.

\* \* \*

It did not take long for Sam and Danielle's marriage to hit the rocks after they exchanged vows in Las Vegas on the

Fourth of July, 1995. Sam hit crack and liquor harder than ever. Danielle threatened to leave him. Very early in the marriage, Sam confided to her his darkest secret. He had already told everyone that Bev left him long ago, back in 1991. That much was common knowledge among Bev's family, Sam's friends, co-workers, even neighbors on Burns Place. But now he told Danielle more.

"I'm going to tell you something that will join us forever," he said. "I killed my first wife."

Later he told her more details: he had strangled Bev in their townhouse. He threw her down the basement stairs. Killed her, dismembered her body, took the parts to Dofasco and dumped them in a vat of molten steel in the department where he worked. And he made it clear the penalty Danielle would pay if she repeated his words to anyone. During one of his crack-fuelled rages, he hung it over Danielle's neck like a sword.

"No one's looking for Bev," he told her. "Why would anyone look for you?"

No one but Danielle would ever really know why she kept the secret in the years that followed. It could simply have been his threat; she saw first hand how violent Sam could be. Or perhaps she feared police might charge her for having said nothing about what she knew. But once he was arrested, and then charged with Maggie Karer's murder, investigators were able to draw Danielle out, get her talking about her past with Sam. Whether it was because she felt safe with Sam in jail, or because she yearned to get back at him for the nightmare of a life he had given her, Danielle revealed the secret.

Her information was a bombshell in the Beverly Davidson case. Given what Peter Abi-Rashed suspected in the Karer homicide, there was symmetry. He had clearly intended to dispose of the body parts in that murder by melting them in molten steel at Dofasco—and apparently it was not the first time. Danielle's revelation had changed everything, but the investigators needed physical evidence to support what she had said. Abi-Rashed called vice and drugs detective Ken Weatherill. Kenny had worked that first night of the case on Easter weekend. He had figured it would be one warrant that night and done. Fifteen warrants later—among them, Burns Place, Sam's white Cougar, his workplace, and the addictions counseling center—he was still at it. Abi told him they needed a new warrant, this time, to get into the townhouses at Barton and Kenora, Unit 38, the last place Sam and Beverly had lived, and the home where Sam told Danielle he killed his first wife.

Weatherill reviewed court documents to prepare the new search warrant in the Beverly Davidson case, in order to make the legal argument why police needed to search the townhouse. He read the petition for divorce Sam had filed, his grab for the kids.

*"The respondent has made no attempt to see the kids."*

Weatherill shook his head as he read Sam's words. Of course "the respondent," Bev, hadn't tried to see her kids, he thought—because you killed her. Weatherill allowed himself to wonder what defense Sam would mount if the Davidson case got to court. On the one hand, Sam's statements while trying to divorce Bev could be seen as arrogant and damning, but on the other, the detective wondered if Sam would use the very brazenness of his filings to his advantage: "Why would I file affidavits like that, openly divorce Bev if I had just killed her? Why risk getting caught like that? Who would do that?"

Gary Yokoyama

Detective Ken Weatherill.

Weatherill wrote a warrant for a property management company at 155 Queen Street North in Hamilton, the company that operated the townhouse complex at Barton Street and Kenora Avenue. Peter Abi-Rashed executed the warrant for the townhouse records on April 14. He learned that only one tenant had lived in Unit 38 in the eight years since Sam and Bev had lived there in 1991. He also hoped to find anyone who used to live near Sam and Beverly in the complex. Did any neighbors see or hear anything unusual, particularly in May 1991?

That afternoon, Abi-Rashed visited the townhouse and met the current tenant of Unit 38, a 25-year-old man, first name Marcin, whose family had Polish roots. He lived in the townhouse with his parents, who were away on an extended vacation. Marcin invited the detective in, happy to assist. Inside, Abi-Rashed stood at the top of the stairs to the basement and peered down, seeing in his mind's eye the story Danielle had relayed. The stairs were narrow and steep, wood painted grey, no carpeting or padding. The stairwell was poorly lit, there was a bulb just inside the door, so when it was turned on, when walking down the stairs you silhouetted yourself, blocking the light, descending into the gloom. At the bottom was a concrete floor painted green.

"We're going to get an official warrant to search the place, Marcin," he said, adding that he could continue living in the unit during the search but could be charged if he interfered in any way.

Abi-Rashed posted a guard 24 hours a day to secure the scene. It was hardly a fresh crime scene—the townhouse unit had already been lived in by at least one other tenant since Sam and Bev were there—but Abi-Rashed was taking no chances. Bottom line, it's tough enough to get a conviction for a homicide; he would not let a lack of attention to detail erode their case. He had been in Major Crime for seven years, but the Karer/Davidson cases had struck a chord with Abi-Rashed. He had learned that you don't let it get to you. He felt the job of a homicide detective is to speak for the deceased, find the guy who did it, put him in jail, and not dwell upon details for longer than necessary. But sometimes you can't help it. Had he become obsessed with the investigation? He didn't like the word, but it fit. Photos of Maggie and Beverly sat on his desk.

"Look at them," he said, holding up the pictures. "Look at them. And this—this bastard—killed them both. And beat them. Beat Beverly repeatedly."

Three Ident officers continued to turn over the scene at Sam Pirrera's home at Burns Place, so a new team was dispatched to the townhouse. Forensic detectives Joe Ridos and Frank Pedersen got the call and reported to Unit 38 on April 19 for a preliminary walk-through. Ridos took notes, documented that the unit had three bedrooms, a bathroom on the second floor; full basement with two parts to it, one part a rec room and the other a laundry/furnace area. "The areas we are going to examine are the basement and bathroom," he wrote.

Like most of his colleagues, Joey Ridos was born and raised in Hamilton. He married Diane, his high school sweetheart, started with the police service in 1979 as a cadet, and had been in forensics for five years. He always wanted to work in Ident branch. On television, forensic detectives often fall into the category of brainy scientist carrying a badge. But the detectives who came up through the Hamilton Ident office were cops who cut their teeth on the street in uniform, and who often were mechanically inclined, a product of their city, Steeltown. They were builders and fixers, but their job involved putting together pieces of puzzles from crime scenes, and deconstructing murder. He loved forensics, in part because he loved working with his hands, like his dad, Joe Sr., who had been a plaster man in Hamilton for years.

Ridos had mixed feelings about having been off work when the initial call came in about body parts found at 12 Burns Place. He couldn't say he was disappointed not to get the hook, but on the other hand, a murder is the ultimate case. Five months earlier he had worked the scene of one of Hamilton's most notorious unsolved homicides, the double-murder of Fred and Lynn Gilbank, found shot to death in their large home in nearby Ancaster.

Ident was back in the townhouse the next day, April 20. They videotaped inside, took photos, and began examining the basement and bathroom with high-intensity light. "Noted was a light spatter type stain on the wallpaper by the stairs at the bottom of the basement floor," Ridos wrote. The stain was tested with a hema stick. "No reaction. Not blood."

That afternoon Abi-Rashed visited the townhouse for a briefing by Ridos and Pedersen. They told him that in the rec-room portion of the basement, wooden paneling had been removed from the walls, and the laundry room had been painted. Abi-Rashed asked the tenant, Marcin, about that. He said that when his family first moved in, the panels had already been removed. On one hand, the detectives knew that was bad news for the investigation—if there had once been blood spatter on the walls, it was long gone. Then again, if Sam had removed the paneling, it could suggest that he had been trying to cover his tracks. But Abi-Rashed knew that what they really needed to find was blood, just a drop, somewhere.

The next day Ridos mixed a batch of luminol at the station. He tested the solution to ensure it worked; usually he would use pigs blood to test; this time he pricked his finger and sprayed his own blood droplets. They shone UV light and an omnichrome light source in the basement and bathroom; the stain noted in the basement in fact had been from water that dripped from the ceiling. The basement windows were covered, luminol sprayed all over, especially the edges of the walls, cracks in floor tiles. They focused on the basement, given what Danielle had relayed about Sam's admission of murdering Bev there, and what Sam appeared to have done in his basement at Burns Place. And, if a dismemberment took place in that unit, it would have happened in the basement; the bathroom was tiny, too small for such an operation.

Three areas of the basement came up with possible blood. One spot turned out to be rust that reacted with the luminol. Another was a drop of paint. Ridos bent down to look more closely at another positive reaction, found on the floor behind a freezer against the wall. He shook his head. There were three or four of them. He shook his head.

"Potato bugs. Dead potato bugs."

Ridos and Pedersen locked the townhouse at 4 p.m. and returned to the station, went upstairs to the Major Crime Unit and told Abi-Rashed the official result of the search was negative. They had found no traces of blood, no sign of a murder, a fight. Ridos handed the key over to him. Abi-Rashed cursed. Yes, it had been a long shot, eight years after Sam and Bev lived there. But it was still a huge letdown. There was still another big shot they had to take, he knew. The one person who knew about Beverly's last moments better than anyone was Sam Pirrera. They needed to talk to him again.

# CHAPTER 18 ~ COLD-BLOODED SWAGGER

The detectives continued cataloguing exhibits and statements in the Maggie Karer homicide. Peter Abi-Rashed met with Ross Wood and Gary Zwicker, going over each bit of evidence, numbering and logging broken bits of glass and wooden furniture from the house, seized items from the basement. Detective Mark Petkoff read all of the statements from witnesses and wrote a brief summary for each on what would be said in court. It was not clear what defense Sam Pirrera would offer. Plead innocence based on some unforeseen alibi? Self-defense? Temporary insanity?

On May 19, Abi-Rashed got a call from James Vincelli, Sam Pirrera's lawyer. At 2:45 p.m. Vincelli met the detectives for a tour of 12 Burns Place. Ident had gutted the basement, every wall and ceiling panel removed, the entire bar dismantled, carpeting gone. The detectives walked Vincelli through the crime scene and offered their account of what had happened in the basement: the assault, beating, blood spatter. They showed him the fruit cellar where the body parts were hidden, and where Constable Kathy Stewart had found the bag and box of remains outside.

Sam Pirrera's next court date wasn't until September 27. There was till time to try and advance the Beverly Davidson case, by taking another crack at Sam in prison. He would have no idea they were coming for an interview. Did Sam know what Danielle had told police about his secret? Might he assume they found evidence of the murder in the old townhouse?

He was no longer at the Barton Street jail. He had requested a transfer to Quinte Penitentiary in Napanee, two hours east of Toronto. At 5:45 a.m. on June 9, Abi-Rashed and Detective Mike Holk hit the highway. The interview this time would be all about Beverly. Abi-Rashed brought a couple of photos with him for Sam to view. He thought they might stimulate some conversation.

Abi-Rashed was optimistic. Since their last interview at Central Station, Sam had had time to dry out, clear his head, get relatively healthy, think about the past and what he had done. He figured Sam had to know they had him cold for Maggie's murder. And so, if he knew he was in for life on that one, maybe he'd admit his role in Bev's death—bring a measure of peace and closure to the Davidson family, and perhaps to Sam as well. Maybe one day his kids could learn the truth, too, about their mother, and find peace as well from that, knowing that she had not just left them as Sam claimed.

After a three-hour drive, Abi-Rashed and Holk arrived at the penitentiary. At 10 a.m., they met with the superintendent, had their ID processed, and talked about the purpose of the visit. Sam's file in prison showed a suicide attempt. He had been the one to request a change of location from Barton jail in Hamilton for his own safety, fearing retribution among the incarcerated—some of whom may have been friends of Maggie Karer's. And yet, in Quinte, he had tried to take his own life, slit his wrists and ankles. He lost a lot of blood and could have died within 30 minutes if staff had not responded quickly. He ended up in physiotherapy to regain movement in one hand after damaging tendons in the wrist.

"I was feeling down and I slit my wrist," he wrote on a prison injury form. "I thought it would end my life."

Abi-Rashed and Holk were escorted to an interview room, sat at a table, and waited for Sam to be brought in. He walked in at 10:18 wearing a blue prisoner jumpsuit. He looked a lot better than the last time Abi-Rashed had seen him, off the crack, eating regularly. He had put on some weight; it showed in his face. The detectives remained sitting when he approached their table. Keep it casual; put Sam at ease. But Sam Pirrera did not sit. He looked down at the detectives.

"How're you doin', Sam?" Abi-Rashed asked.

"OK."

"How are things?"

"OK."

"Anyone from the family come visit?"

"Couple of times."

"It's a long drive for them."

"Yeah."

"Was your idea to come here, though, eh?"

"Yeah."

Sam had still not sat down. Abi-Rashed slipped a photo from a folder and placed it on the table in front of him: Beverly.

"We came here to talk to you about Bev," he said.

"Talk to my lawyer."

And with that Sam Pirrera slowly turned, calmly walked out of the room, and never once looked back. Abi-Rashed was stunned. Looked at his watch: 10:20. The exchange took less than two minutes. He turned to Holk.

"What the—what just happened?"

He shut them down before they even started. You show up to talk to an accused, he might not want to talk, might cut off the conversation at some point. Might even take a swing at you. But he does not walk out like that. With Sam Pirrera, there was no denial, no anger, nothing. Just that cocky attitude, a cold-blooded swagger. *I will talk when I choose.* In all his years, dealing with the worst of humanity, Abi-Rashed had never seen a man charged with murder behave like that.

"I drove four hours for that? Do you believe that?"

"So now what do you want to do?" Holk asked.

"Get breakfast, I guess."

And they did. Abi had bacon and eggs, over easy. Then the long drive back to Hamilton, just in time to hit plodding rush-hour Toronto traffic for good measure, Peter Abi-Rashed at the wheel, still roasting mad, expletives flying most of the way.

* * *

On September 27, Sam Pirrera appeared in a Hamilton court and waived his right to a preliminary hearing in the murder of Maggie Karer. His lawyer, James Vincelli, conceded there was sufficient evidence to commit Sam to trial. And Beverly? Abi-Rashed still had no crime scene, no body. No statement of any kind from Pirrera on the matter, much less a confession. But what he did have was a list of circumstantial evidence and he felt that, when taken together, it all offered a case for charging him with her murder as well:

Exhibits in the Maggie Karer case.

- Clearly Sam had tried to cover up Bev's disappearance, telling friends and Bev's family lies about her moving to California. The detectives had even found the woman who had three times phoned the Davidson home, claiming to be Bev, in California—the woman admitted to police that Sam put her up to it. She was a crack addict. She did what Sam told her to do.

- Sam had a long history of abusing Bev and other women in his life. One woman, a prostitute, told police that one day she got in Sam's car, and when she tried to leave, he started beating on her but she managed to escape and run away on the street.

- Sam had actually told Danielle he killed Bev, cut her up, and put her parts in molten scrap metal at Dofasco.

Danielle had shown police she was a credible source on the Karer murder. Her information on the Beverly Davidson murder and dismemberment paralleled aspects of the Maggie Karer case—Sam had dipped Maggie's body parts in gasoline, had tried to get to Dofasco, just as he told Danielle he had done with his first wife.

- Not only had Sam told Danielle his secret about Bev, but over the years he had, when high on crack or drunk on booze, spoken loosely to several people about "how to get rid of someone"—he would actually talk like that, detectives learned through interviews. It may have sounded simply like sick humor at the time, this talk about cutting someone up and burning the parts at the steel company where he worked. But now, in the context of everything else he had said and done, it carried damning weight.

- There was something else: the detectives had received information from someone who once lived in the townhouses at Barton and Kenora about noises heard in Sam and Bev's unit. Sounds of a brutal struggle around the time Beverly went missing. The statement meshed with what Danielle had told them about what he had done to Beverly.

Abi-Rashed wanted to charge Sam with the second murder and had to sell that notion to the Crown. In January 2000, he met with a Hamilton assistant Crown attorney named Fred Campling, who had been assigned to prosecute the Maggie Karer homicide. Abi-Rashed had laid out his reasons to Campling why he felt that charges should be added against Sam for Beverly's death.

Fred Campling had been prosecuting cases in Hamilton for 22 years. Four years earlier, he had turned the key on Jon

Rallo, convincing a jury to reject the triple-murderer's attempt to get early parole. He had recently come off working the case of a Canadian soldier charged with stealing handguns from a Hamilton armory and trading them for crack cocaine—the case ended prematurely when the soldier hanged himself with a bed sheet at the Quinte Detention Centre. And, late in 1998, Campling had prosecuted a man who killed an American bus driver who was passing through town and staying at the Admiral Inn. The killer, along with a teenage accomplice, bashed the driver over the head repeatedly with a lamp after a sexual liaison and then robbed him.

Campling, who was 50 years old, had a staid, measured manner, careful with every syllable he uttered in court, or to the media. His mom and dad had been teachers; his father taught at Royal Military College and Queen's University in Kingston, Ont. Fred was born in Boston while his dad was on a teaching job in that city, but he grew up in Kingston. Fred attended M.I.T. for civil engineering, and ultimately attended law school at Queen's.

Campling had a compact frame; he kept fit by swimming every morning. He wasn't a strong swimmer, certainly not very fast, but he reflected that it was an activity for which he didn't require any motivation. He always dressed sharp, kept his office in spartan condition. He had a gentlemanly, understated aura about him, but below the surface lurked a tough and relentless prosecutor. He left nothing to chance, and that included not tipping his hand about what made him tick. On the surface, at least, the buttoned-down Campling was a contrast to Peter Abi-Rashed's booming personality. The detective was going full-bore, great guns to charge Sam Pirrera for double murder, and the assistant Crown attorney calmed him down, trying to ensure all the ducks were in a row.

Towards the end of 1999 and early in 2000, pre-trial nego-tiations on a plea deal continued between Sam's lawyer, James

Vincelli, and Campling. Other cases on Vincelli's plate of late included defending a man charged in a machete-wielding assault, and a repressed-memory case where he defended an elderly man against charges of abuse by a woman 23 years after the alleged abuse occurred.

On January 27, Abi-Rashed met again with Campling, who instructed Abi-Rashed to lay a new charge of second-degree murder against Sam Pirrera in Beverly Davidson's death. In Abi-Rashed's white homicide notebook, he had written of the "J. Doe" homicide, which had become the "Karer homicide." And now, after many more pages and notes of hits and misses, he wrote, finally: "Karer/Davidson homicide."

On the Maggie Karer homicide alone, the Crown could almost certainly win a first-degree murder conviction. But the focus was on bringing the deaths of both women together and obtaining Sam's admission of responsibility for each. Abi-Rashed was pleased for the families; there would be no drawn-out trial with gory details splashed all over the media, no appeal process. The families would have justice and closure. Win-win for everyone.

The deal struck was that Sam would plead guilty to second-degree murder in both cases, and the life sentences would run concurrently. What was in it for Sam? Second-degree murder would make him eligible for parole in 10 years instead of the 25 years that comes with first-degree murder, although, given the nature of the crimes, the chances were slim he'd get parole. And, Abi-Rashed allowed himself to wonder, perhaps even Sam Pirrera would find a measure of peace in owning up to what he did—for his kids, for himself.

For Abi-Rashed, as a veteran investigator, it was gratifying. Not often do you get a double-murder charge when you are missing one of the bodies. The investigative team had logged a lot of hours, seen things they would never forget; it was the worst case they had experienced. But they did the job. The guys who worked the case had moved on to other cases and branches with the service. Wayne Bennett, who had played a lead role early on and conducted key interviews with people who had knowledge of Pirrera throughout the investigation, decided to return to uniform patrol, give himself a chance to clean up his remaining court cases before retiring. It was the first time he had worn the uniform since 1983. He still had the raspy voice and thousand-yard stare, and so the uniform suited him. Once again he was just a cop with a tight haircut and a long memory.

The uniformed cop who was first on the scene when the case blew open, Kathy Stewart, fulfilled her dream. The Pirrera case had given her a taste of investigative work; she vowed to become a detective. And she did, eventually getting promoted to a detective position in the service's Criminal Investigation Division.

Senior Ident man Ross Wood retired soon after his work on the Karer homicide was done. One day he got home from work, looked at his wife, Marjory, and just knew. "That's it," he said. It wasn't the Pirrera case that drove him out. In fact he found it quite interesting. It wasn't the blood and gore of crime scenes in general, either. It was more the politics, and seeing criminals walk free on a technicality, or working all night at a scene then rushing to court, into the witness box, to argue with lawyers. He loved golf, and so took a summer job working at Heron Point golf club, a jewel of a place. Woody worked as an on-course marshal, ensuring the golfers play quickly enough. "I'm the guy you keep looking over your shoulder for, hoping I don't come around."

# Chapter 19 ~ Cell 4231

Sam was scheduled to appear in court in January 2000 to hear the new charges read for the murders of both Maggie and Bev. The media would be all over the new angle, that Sam Pirrera had allegedly murdered his first wife. That meant the police needed to notify the families of the news. Victim Services branch at the Hamilton Police Service had special concern for Bev and Sam's children, Ashlee and Matthew, who were now 12 and nine.

Ashlee Pirrera had been asking questions about her father ever since she heard that he was arrested. A social worker with the Hamilton Catholic School Board had been assigned to help back in April right after he went to jail. Her name was Ola Furda, a 48-year-old woman who was born and raised in Toronto, and whose parents were from the Ukraine. Ola had studied psychology at York University, and after graduation went out west, to Calgary, where she worked in the criminal courts. She thought she wanted to become a Justice of the Peace. But she spent some time with hard luck cases in the system, and also spent time visiting native reservations, including the Blood Reserve in Southern Alberta, that opened her eyes to poverty she had never experienced before. She decided to go back east and study social work at McMaster University in Hamilton.

Ola could not simply answer Ashlee's questions straight, reveal all the details that had been reported in the media. So far, Ashlee's grandparents, Lina and Antonio Pirrera, Sam's parents, had told Ashlee that her father was in jail for doing something wrong—just what, she was not told. She had not yet learned anything close to the truth about what Sam was accused of doing to Maggie Karer.

Ashlee tried to sneak peeks at the newspaper for answers, and eavesdropped on conversations in her family, but she was never sure who or what to believe. Later it became apparent that her grandparents were feeding her false information about what her father was accused of doing. Mostly, through the spring and summer of 1999, she wanted to believe the best about him, even though she knew first hand of Sam Pirrera's rage and capacity for violence when abusing drugs and alcohol. She feared that he would stay in jail and that, eventually, she would not be able to see him at all. She visited him in jail and saw bandages covering his wrists and hands. Sam told Ashlee he had accidentally hurt himself. During the visit he did not seem quite like himself; he had been sedated.

Ola Furda's sessions with the two kids in April and into May was a crisis intervention to help them cope, and get them going to school. They had not wanted to attend, worried that kids would tease them about their jailed father. Ashlee stayed inside at recess, avoiding comments on the playground. A couple of kids teased them, but the attention died down when media coverage of the case temporarily waned. In the summer of 1999, Ola sent them to a Tim Hortons camp out east in Nova Scotia; she felt it did wonders for them to get away.

When the new school year started in the fall of 1999, Ola continued to help, developing a bond with Ashlee. Ola thought of herself as a no-bull social worker. She gave it straight to her, and Ashlee responded well to the tough love. One day, she saw that Ashlee had dyed her hair with three colors, and raised an eyebrow.

"C'mon Ash," Ola said.

"You kind of nag a lot," Ashlee said with a grin.

"Of course I do," Ola replied.

"You don't like the hair?"

"No, I don't."

Another time, Ashlee relayed to Ola that a boy she liked was being mean to her, acting like a jerk, but she still wanted to hang out with him. "Why take crap like that?" Ola said. "Don't you respect yourself?"

Ola could tell from the start that Ashlee was an intelligent and strong girl who had been forced to grow up in a hurry. True, she was still in denial about her father, but that was understandable, given the mixed messages she had been receiving. Ola asked Ashlee about her biological mother, Bev, who the girl had barely known, and was no longer around.

"My mom left us a long time ago," Ashlee said. She was still angry about that, a mother just abandoning them like that. It was what she had been told all her life. Her perception about that was all about to dramatically change. In late January 2000, an officer with Hamilton Police Victim Services contacted Ola. She needed to prepare the kids for news that was about to break about a new charge against their father. Right before the story went public, Ola met the kids at school and sat down with them in a private room.

"I have some really bad news," Ola began. "Although in some ways it will answer some questions you have about your biological mother. You mother did not abandon you. Your father has been charged with murdering her."

Ola did not go into detail about what the police suspected, that Sam had dismembered Bev's body just as he had with Maggie. But that day, everything changed for Ashlee. She no longer wanted to believe the best about her father. She loved him, he was her father, but now at the same time she hated him. For a time she also went through a period where she wondered if her mom was still alive. Maybe, she thought, her dad was just crazy, and he didn't really do all the things he told people he did. *We need to get more people out there looking for her!*

Over time, though, Ashlee came to believe that her father had killed Bev. And from the moment she knew that her mother had not in fact abandoned them, she felt an over-whelming sense of guilt for having ever believed it all those years. She kept thinking back to how she felt growing up; she knew that she had always had some sense in her heart that it didn't add up. Even as a little girl, it didn't make sense that her mom would leave, she just had a feeling.

The guilt turned to anger, at herself, and at everyone else for lying to her. She increasingly questioned the answers she had been given by her grandparents, Lina and Antonio Pirrera. And she was only 12 years old. She started to hear voices, have flashbacks: she was standing up in a crib, a lady is there, who it is, she doesn't know, but then her father storms into the room and drags her out.

At times, Ashlee wondered what her own future held, the teasing from kids at school now ringing in her ears. She was the daughter of a killer.

"Am I going to be like him?" she asked Ola.

"No. You are nothing like him," Ola replied. "You are spiritual, nothing like him. You do not share the life experiences he has had. And your mother is a part of you, too."

Ashlee and Ola had spirited conversations. Ola let the girl vent about everything that was happening in her life. It seemed to give her strength. But neither of them could be prepared for what was still to come, for what Sam Pirrera was still capable of doing.

* * *

On January 28, Sam appeared in a Hamilton courtroom to hear the new charges read for the murders of Maggie Karer and Beverly Davidson. He was remanded in custody and transported back to Quinte penitentiary until February 18, when he would appear in court again to officially enter a plea, and assistant Crown attorney Fred Campling would speak to the case.

Gary Yokoyama

Pirrera was charged with two murders.

Peter Abi-Rashed wrote the date in his notebook and triple-underlined it. As the day approached he felt the pressure building, consumed by the case day and night. He made security arrangements for the February 18 court date, private entrances and exits and police escorts, so that Maggie's and Bev's families would be kept from the media horde that he knew would be there.

He met often with Campling and helped prepare the narrative for the prosecutor to read in court, describing the sequence of events and evidence. It seemed like every time they met it was pitch black outside, always after 5 p.m., late January when the days are short and dark. They talked about how they would handle explaining the plea deal to Maggie's and Bev's families, who would say what, how to make the conversation go as smoothly as possible, with no one left feeling bitter or confused.

They met with Margaret Karer, Maggie's mother, on February 9, and with Lesa Davidson the next day. They talked to each mother about the deal, gave it to them straight, the good and the bad: no, it won't be a life sentence, but there will be admission of guilt and closure for everyone. The mothers could have chosen to reject the strategy, but they did not. They wanted first-degree murder, but understood that the plea would finally end it. Maggie and Beverly could rest in peace, and Sam would finally take responsibility for what he had done. Still, the conversations with Abi-Rashed and Campling were emotional, intense.

"All I want," said one of the mothers, her voice shaking with emotion, "is to be able to stand up in court and look him in the eye and ask him why? Why?" With the plea deal, the mothers would not have the chance to take the stand, but would be able say their piece in court through their victim impact statements.

Everything had fallen into place. They were all set for the big day, February 18.

"Showtime," thought Abi-Rashed.

*  *  *

*Saturday, Feb. 12, 2000*
*11:20 a.m.*
*Toronto East Detention Centre*

The chemical snaked through the 32-year-old inmate's bloodstream, winding its way to his brain, binding to receptors. Shortly after injecting heroin the user feels a surge of euphoria. A warm flush of the skin. Dry mouth. The inmate reached for the piece of fruit left over from a snack, felt the smooth texture of the pear. He likely felt a heavy feeling in the arms and legs: sleepy, then suddenly awake, and sleepy again. Mind clouding, can't think straight. A bit of nausea, itchy skin. Can't get air, the brain's signals to the lungs retarded, can't breathe, suffocating.

And then? Unspeakably bloody visions in his mind's eye fading from red to black? A kaleidoscope of people and places and love and hate and rage? A sense of relief—or worse, sudden regret? Or maybe none of that: simply a plain jail cell wall growing paler and paler, moving closer, covering him like a blanket. It all wouldn't have taken more than several minutes. He did not respond to the breakfast call. He lay still on the top bunk in Cell 4231. The pear rested in Sam Pirrera's cold hand.

Gary Yokoyama

Toronto East Detention Centre.

\* \* \*

On Saturday, February 12, Abi-Rashed was off the clock. No jacket or tie, just jeans, a casual shirt. That afternoon he drove from his home down the Mountain to the east end to visit a friend. He didn't stay long, left the house, walked down the front steps toward his navy blue LeSabre parked on the road. He squinted into the sun. It was cold out, but a crisp and beautiful blue-sky day. He would never forget it.

Beep. Beep.

His pager. He got into his car and called the number back on his cell.

"Abi-Rashed," he said.

He listened to the words.

Gary Yokoyama

"Yeah, right," he replied, and hung up.

Beep. Beep.

He called the number again.

"Abi," the voice said. "Don't hang up. Listen."

And he did, the blood draining from his face. The bastard. It was over.

Detective-Sergeant Abi-Rashed couldn't believe it.

# Chapter 20 ~ A Higher Court

That afternoon, Ashlee sat at her grandma Lina Pirrera's kitchen table eating lunch. Sam's mother kept the family home spotless, impossibly clean, plastic coverings on some of the furniture. Ashlee's toddler half-sister, Sam and Danielle's daughter, was also over visiting at the house on Cannon Street. Ashlee had been continuing to meet with her social worker, Ola Furda, and tried turning to her faith as her father awaited his next court date on a double murder charge, including the murder of Ashlee's mother. She said her prayers every night. Please make sure everyone is OK, she would say at the end of the prayers, and, after everyone else was covered, she'd say a little prayer for herself, asking that her life be normal, just for once.

"Please help me, just give me a break. Just one."

Her attendance at church had been spotty though. Whenever she saw her old priest, Father Mark, he would give her the look: *Are you going to church?* One day back in December, she walked past Blessed Sacrament Church, stopped, entered, and offered a confession for the first time in a while. She started to attend in January with a friend and enjoyed it, even though church, and God, had let her down before. She was willing to give it another shot, start the new year fresh.

The phone rang in the kitchen at the Pirrera home. Lina answered it, and then her face broke. She left the room and walked upstairs, pacing back and forth. Ashlee could hear the footsteps. What? What is going on? And then a family member told her the news. The sandwich she was holding fell to the floor. Ashlee felt numb, emotions she could not categorize rippled through her. She didn't want pity from anyone. She didn't want anything.

\* \* \*

"Pirrera is dead."

The words over his cell hit Peter Abi-Rashed like a hammer. He cursed aloud, could not believe what he was hearing from an officer at Central Station. No. Can't be. This was not how it works. Abi-Rashed had been meticulous in overseeing his team's investigation, working with the Crown, the families. He had his man, game over. Sam was due in court in six days, expected to plead guilty to both murders, everyone was ready—and what?

"What the—what happened?"

"Looks like an overdose."

"Overdose?" Abi-Rashed said. "How?"

He learned that Sam had been found dead in his cell at Toronto East Detention Centre, after having been transferred from the penitentiary in Quinte, as a stopover en route to appearing in Hamilton court. He had been in the Toronto jail less than 24 hours.

Abi-Rashed drove towards Central Station. They were not getting their day in court. Why couldn't the bastard have waited a week before doing himself? Abi-Rashed's slow drive along King Street towards the station was surreal. It seemed to last forever, the lower city bathed in a golden glow from the sun. For a moment his instinctive skepticism kicked in. Maybe there had been a mix-up, maybe it was a different Pirrera. And Toronto East Detention? What the hell was he doing there in the first place? Sam had been at Quinte Detention Centre. Shouldn't Barton Street jail have been his next stop before his court date?

The detective wondered later if, at the moment he heard the news, he felt hatred towards Sam Pirrera. If so, that would be a first. You deal with nasty characters in homicide but Abi-Rashed did his job; he did not hate. What he felt was ripped off. *They had a deal.* Long ago, little Sam had thumbed his nose at Abi-Rashed on the streets of north Hamilton back in his teens, and much later after graduating to the most heinous crimes, had shut him down at the Quinte interview in June, literally turning his back on him. And now this.

"He did it to me again," Abi-Rashed said.

Later, he stared at his white homicide casebook, packed with a day-by-day account of the investigation since Easter weekend 1999. He had written notes on his meetings with the families leading up to the big February 18 court date. And then, on the next page, where his account of those proceedings should have begun, he saw—nothing. Not a word. Blank.

All he could do now was try to help the families. He sent three police cruisers to the Karer and Davidson homes to pass along the news before they heard about it on the news. He called other officers from the investigative team. He phoned Ross Wood. "Pirrera has pleaded guilty," Abi-Rashed said. "He's gone to a higher court."

Detective Wayne Bennett, who had been Abi-Rashed's lead investigator on the ground, turned over all his Pirrera case notebooks to him. "Pirrera had the last say, as it turned out," Bennett said. Benny had been around long enough not to be all that surprised about the fatal overdose. He knew inmates smuggle as much drugs into jail as they can get away with. Prison staffers do what they can to police it. But where there's a will, there's a way. Detective Mark Petkoff read about it in a newspaper when he was at a Hamilton hockey arena, where his son was refereeing a game. Pirrera dead. What goes around, comes around, he thought.

On February 14, Abi-Rashed stood behind a lectern for a news conference at the police station. This was his chance to roll out what they had not made public before. Without going into all the details, he outlined the case against Sam Pirrera, particularly for the murder of his first wife, Beverly.

"What about the motive behind the murders?" a reporter asked.

"We will never know," Abi-Rashed said. "Only Sam Pirrera has that answer."

Abi-Rashed's anger was palpable in the room, his body language rigid, his dark eyes burning. He knew this was not how it was supposed to go, not how Major Crime investigative work is supposed to be put on display. Detectives collect evidence, build a case for presentation to the Crown, in court—not for the media. Abi-Rashed didn't like revealing information to reporters at the best of times. He hated how the investigation, his investigation, had been short-circuited and reduced to a press conference, denied the proper forum in court to test their case. It was all wide-open now for any civilian to chip away at what they had gathered, second-guess, speculate. For Abi-Rashed, driven, by the book to the core, it was torture.

Sam would never admit or deny anything for the record. No one would ever know what he might have said once he got into a courtroom. His lawyer, James Vincelli, would never offer reporters any comment about the case, or about Sam Pirrera. Solicitor-client privilege. He could never betray what Sam told him. All he would say was that, yes, a plea deal offer was made, but as far as the anticipated guilty plea went, "Until someone appears in court and actually does something, it's just speculation."

In *The Hamilton Spectator,* a spokesman for Dofasco questioned the validity of the evidence that suggested Sam had dumped Beverly's body parts in a vat of molten steel: "It's a police theory that has never been confirmed. They have a theory that is somewhat speculative. Under the circumstances I don't think anyone will be able to uncover all of the facts. It certainly appears [that Sam] was a sadly disturbed individual."

* * *

Sam Pirrera's body was split open on an examination table, organs removed, tissue samples sliced off, placed in jars. When an inmate dies in custody there is by law an autopsy, investigation, and coroner's inquest. Dr. Bruce Walker, a toxicologist with the Centre of Forensic Sciences in Toronto, examined fluid samples collected at the autopsy, femoral blood from the leg, blood from the heart, urine, stomach contents. He studied samples from the liver, hair. The blood in the heart showed a concentration of morphine of 10,000 nanograms per milliliter. Morphine is a product of the metabolism of heroin in the body. Death can occur with concentrations as low as 200 ng/ml. The amount in Sam's blood was the highest Walker had ever seen in his career, or in any of the literature. It was enough to kill several men. Heroin can be smoked, inhaled through the nose, taken orally, or injected.

The overdose was either heroin or pure morphine, most likely heroin, Walker deduced: "Death would have come rapidly." There could be no doubt that the overdose came in his Toronto cell. He had been transported from Quinte to Toronto East Detention about 24 hours earlier, mid-morning on Friday, February 11. It was to be a brief stopover before transport to Barton Street jail.

Later, the inquest began in Toronto. The question of why he wasn't watched more closely at the jail in Toronto was explored, among others. His suicidal tendencies had been documented in his file ever since his arrest in Hamilton at St. Joseph's Hospital, where he tried to kill himself. At the Quinte Detention Centre a small needle had been found in his cell; he had also attempted suicide by cutting himself there, and told prison staff he wanted to do it on more than one occasion. He had asked inmates how to get drugs to do the job. And still his capacity for violence had not waned; at the time of his death he was on probation for an assault that occurred in custody.

Despite all this, a psychiatrist at Quinte had opined two weeks before he was transferred to Toronto that Sam had "zero suicidal ... and zero threatening" thoughts. These opinions were included in his chart for Toronto East Detention Centre staff. When he was transferred, guards in Toronto found a cut latex glove in an empty Player's cigaret package among his personal belongings. Drug-smuggling inmates cut the fingers off latex gloves and wrap drugs for smuggling in body cavities. Still, he was placed in the jail's general population instead of a segregated unit for suicidal prisoners, and he was never spoken to by medical staff there.

The only indisputable fact of his death was that it was caused by a massive overdose. But more questions than answers hung out there. How was the lethal dose administered? Did Sam get help? Did he ingest it orally, as pills or liquid form, and if so, how could he have smuggled so much of the drug into his cell?

Bruce Walker believed that Pirrera injected the drug. It would account for the high concentration found in the heart— five times more—in contrast to the lower amount in the leg. Injection brings death quickly. The heart pumps the drug to the brain, where it has its major impact. Moreover, an examination of stomach contents showed no presence of fragments of capsules or tablets. Given the size of the overdose, had Sam taken it orally, there would have been evidence of that.

And yet, in some ways, it did not add up. No needle marks were found on his body. And there was no syringe, needle, or any drug paraphernalia spotted in his cell. What did it all mean? Had Sam meant to commit suicide? Had he taken more drug than he intended? Was another person involved? Perhaps the needle hole was in a crevice that was simply not visible upon examination. Perhaps he had flushed the needle down the toilet before dying, although he would not have had much time. Or, the search of the cell simply had not been thorough.

The inquest held in a Toronto courtroom had an oddly detached feel to it. Journalists attending said it felt rushed, as though officials were going through the motions, examining the untimely death of a man for whom there was no sympathy. No one from the victims' families attended, nor did anyone from Sam's family, including his ex-wife, Danielle. She had not been surprised to hear the news of his death. She said that Sam had once told her that if he was ever put away in jail, he would do himself in.

After hearing testimony from jail guards, the toxicologist, coroner, and other officials, a six-member inquest jury deliberated in private to make a recommendation based on what they had heard. One of the jurors, Arno Koppel, a retired dairy worker, thought the discussion was all so much nonsense. Nothing much they could say would stop an inmate from killing himself in the future if he really wanted to. As for the cause of death, he felt it was probably a suicide. But the details weren't all that relevant. The bottom line was Pirrera was dead, and rightly so.

"The best thing that could have happened to a person like that is to die," he said. "He is useless in society." One of the jury's recommendations was that in the future, jails should conduct prompt medical assessments on mentally ill inmates. The jury's official verdict on the death of Sam Pirrera was narcotic toxicity caused by suicide.

For all the exploration of how Sam was treated at the jail and the preventative measures that could have been taken, a Toronto detective who investigated the death suggested there was in the end not much that could have been done. "Even if he had been on suicide watch," said Colin Sinclair, "he could have still done what he did."

Back in Hamilton, there would always be those who believed that Sam had been murdered. A friend of Maggie Karer's
said she received a phone call a couple of weeks prior to Sam's
death. The caller had connections with some rough characters
and some of them were in jail, men who knew Maggie from
the street and were furious at Sam Pirrera for what he had
done. "Within two weeks Pirrera will be dead, that's the word
on the street," the caller said. Sam himself feared retribution
in prison; it was the reason he asked that he be transferred
to Quinte from Barton jail. But, apart from questions about
the exact manner of overdose, there was little evidence to
support the murder theory.

The inquest heard evidence gathered from Sam's cell mate
at Quinte that suggested Sam's increased desire to end his life
seemed to coincide with the new charges filed against him in
January 2000 for Bev's murder. This was the point at which he
seemed depressed, jittery, very quiet, when he talked about
there being no light at the end of the tunnel, that he wanted
to find a way out.

But no one could know what was going on inside Sam
Pirrera's head, and no psychological profile of him was ever
done—there was no need for Hamilton Police to ask for one:
they had caught him, and he agreed to plead guilty. There
was to be no plea of insanity that would have necessitated
psychiatric analysis. If he was prepared to enter a guilty plea
and take responsibility for the deaths of Bev and Maggie, why
commit suicide before he could make it official in court? Why
not wait? Why not at least attempt the road to some measure
of redemption? He was only 32 years old. The notion of a
"jittery" Sam Pirrera desperate to end his pain fit with the
general profile of a crack addict, but at the same time did not
fit with the calculation he had shown in his life and crimes,
and with the way he snubbed police at Quinte.

Perhaps suicide on the eve of his confession was his
way of spitting in the face of everyone at the moment of

his choosing—the cops, the women who left him. It was a final turn of his back on the world at which he had always raged. No one leaves Sam Pirrera. *You're not going anywhere.* This time, he would do the leaving. He would decide.

There was one question that Peter Abi-Rashed turned over in his head and, on this one, he was not about to let Sam's soul rest. The man kills and dismembers two women in cold blood, eight years apart—eight years without trying it again? The detective wondered if there were other victims out there. Sam had not yet provided police with a DNA sample, and so Abi-Rashed decided to get one post-mortem. Prior to the autopsy, he asked a coroner to draw an extra blood sample from the body. It was a highly unusual step for police. Sam Pirrera's DNA profile remained on record for future investigations, just in case.

# Chapter 21 ~ Scars

Samuel Joseph Pirrera's body lay in the open casket in Friscolanti's Funeral Chapel, eyes looking down upon him as the long procession of people shuffled along. The body was dressed in a black suit, and in death his face still showed a shadow of beard. The funeral chapel was on Barton Street East, the area where Sam grew up and ran from police as a teenager. The chapel was packed for the visitation, friends of the Pirrera family and members of the Italian community.

Sam's mother wept, while his kids, Ashlee and her younger brother, Matthew, showed no tears, their faces blank, looking utterly lost. Ola Furda, the social worker who had been meeting regularly with the kids, arrived and passed by the coffin. She looked at Sam's face and felt a mix of fear, relief, and disbelief. How could he have done the things he did, and lived with those secrets for so long? And then, on top of it all, he kills himself, causing his kids even more pain. A selfish act, she thought; he just didn't want to live in jail. Ola reflected that perhaps Sam did not possess a conscience. She felt a bit hypocritical being there "paying respects," but then she also knew that's not why she came, that it was only for the children, to support them.

On Thursday, February 17, the funeral was held at St. Patrick's church, the coffin covered with a white cloth and topped with red and white carnations. Family of both Maggie and Bev were appalled that he received most of the full Catholic funeral rites. Three years earlier, notorious Hamilton mobster Johnny (Pops) Papalia had been denied the same rites after he was shot dead on Railway Street. How could Sam be worthy of it? And by Catholic tradition, if he had committed suicide, didn't that also preclude him from receiving full rites?

The chancellor of the Diocese of Hamilton, Father Gerard Bergie, defended the funeral for Sam Pirrera at the time. Years ago, suicide was indeed a disqualification for full funeral rites in the Catholic Church, but no longer. The church now saw suicide as an illness, not so much a choice of the individual, he argued. As for Sam's crimes, Bergie acknowledged their heinous nature. But, he said, a Christian funeral is not meant as a celebration of the deceased, contrary to what many think. "It is a focus on eternal life, and what awaits us: judgment. In the liturgy we are commending him to God, and God is the ultimate judge." Years after the funeral, however, Bergie acknowledged that there are occasions—and Pops Papalia's funeral had been one of them—where the service can be altered to account for a person of truly notorious actions. He would have suggested something other than full rites for Sam, if he had known the extent of the crimes at the time.

As for Sam Pirrera's destination in the next world, Bergie believed in hell as a place defined by the absence of God, being completely cut off from Him, and the pain and suffering that comes from that. "We can't judge what will happen in the afterlife. But we can judge actions, and no question his were abhorrent to what we stand for as human beings."

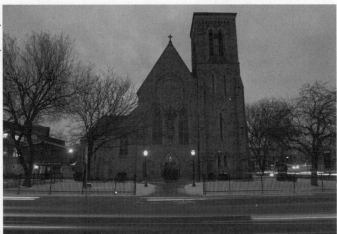

Gary Yokoyama

Sam's funeral was held at St. Patrick's church.

After the ceremony in church, the Pirrera family stood over the open grave at Holy Sepulchre Cemetery just outside Hamilton, the day turning cloudy and cold. It was the same section of the cemetery where the remains of Maggie Karer and her father, Les Karer, lay. Ashlee, who was 12, had never even been to a funeral before, and now it hit her: this wasn't some ceremony in church, something symbolic: this was really happening, her father, jailed for murdering two women, including her mother, was being buried. Like the others standing there, she held a rose in her hand. The roses started falling, dropping onto the casket as it sank lower, and Ashlee let go of hers. She might have been crying, or not. She could never remember.

Ashlee continued asking questions about exactly what her father had done to her mother. She felt that her grandparents, Lina and Antonio Pirrera, continued to keep the truth from her. Ashlee found a copy of the *The Hamilton Spectator* in their basement and scanned an article. The newspaper ran a feature story documenting more details about the investigation into Bev's disappearance, including the belief of police that Sam had murdered and dismembered her, dumping her parts in molten steel. Ashlee asked her grandparents about what was being written. She was told they were all lies. She didn't know what to think, and she was also denied access to her Nana, Lesa Davidson, Bev's mom, who could have told her more about what the police had relayed her way. As for Ola Furda, she collected all of the articles; she knew that one day she would review them with Ashlee, when the time was right. She wanted to protect her, but at the same time, did not want her hearing lies. Ola urged the grandparents to be careful about what they told Ashlee—and that included not feeding her false information, which would be just as damaging in the long run.

Two months later, on Saturday, April 8, on a damp and cold day that started with rain and later snowed, a memorial was held for Bev at the White Chapel Memorial Gardens on Main Street West. There were flowers and a photo collage at the ceremony; there could be no burial, not when her remains were gone. Bev's sister-in-law, Lori, and her childhood friend Karen, had gone to the library, found some poetry, and read passages aloud at the service: "They are not dead; those loved ones who have passed beyond our vision for a little while. They have reached the light while we still grope in darkness where we can't see them smile. But smile they do, and love us and do not forget nor ever go so far away."

Bev's memorial stone.

It was a simple service, a couple of dozen people attended, including police officers. But Bev's kids were not among them. Ola Furda asked Lina Pirrera if the could attend, but she said absolutely not, she did not want them to go: it wasn't necessary, they had never had a relationship with their mother, she argued. They didn't remember her; it would have been too hard on them. The kids were angry about it. Lesa Davidson, who had held out hope of gaining custody of Bev's children, seethed about it all.

"It's their mother and I think they should have been here," she told the *Spectator*. "If they have to grieve for their father they can grieve for their mother, too."

The kids were denied even knowing where Bev's memorial stone lay, but for a long time, the Pirrera grandparents would take the kids to Sam's gravesite, every single week. Ashlee would stare at his stone, which had a color picture inset of Sam in a white tuxedo and red tie, and she would often cry.

And still, for Ashlee, with everything that had come before, it was not long after her father died that she confronted another horror in her young life. She had continued to live with her grandparents, Sam's parents. And her grandfather started to abuse her, after Sam had killed himself. She had trusted her grandfather completely, grown close, and now she would lie awake in the dark in her father's old house, dreading the sound of her grandfather's footsteps up the stairs. She told her grandmother about it and was told to lock her bedroom door.

The abuse was the last straw. She had benefited so much from her conversations with Ola Furda, but now she lost it. She felt like the last remnant of her faith was gone, just like both her parents. She had kept praying for everyone to just be OK, and no one was OK. She had prayed for one break in life, just once. But no. She stopped praying and now felt like she just didn't want to continue. What did she have to live for, she wondered? She felt like she was losing her mind. One day, she felt the blood on her skin, as she dug a sharp edge into her wrists.

Something stopped her. The injuries were only superficial. Ola felt it was Ashlee's spirituality, weakened though it had been; the teenager had such strong faith, even knew elements of Catholic theology with which Ola herself was not familiar. One day, Ashlee, who was in Grade 9, saw Ola driving by just outside Cathedral high school, which she now attended. She flagged Ola down. She stopped the car, rolled down her window, and Ashlee bent down and looked at her.

"I have something important to tell you," Ashlee said.

Ashlee had confided in a friend about her grandfather's abuse, and the friend had insisted that she report it. Do it, or else I will, the friend told her. And now she did. Ola parked her car and walked Ashlee to the Children's Aid Society office. They took a shortcut, walking across Cathedral's football field, and right in the door. She was immediately taken out of the Pirrera home and placed with a foster family. Sam's father, Antonio Pirrera, was charged with three counts each of sexual assault and sexual interference against her. He was given a six-month conditional sentence and ordered not to communicate or associate with Ashlee "directly or indirectly" and not be in the company of any female child under 16. In her victim impact statement, Ashlee said she would never trust her grandfather again, and that her relationship with her 11-year-old brother was destroyed by the case: "He told me he didn't believe me…My family now seems divided into the people who believe me and the people who don't. It hurts that they've known me my whole life, and now when something serious has happened, it's as if some of them don't care anymore."

With everything bad in her life snowballing, Ashlee felt like she was losing it, but at the same time she had not turned to drinking or drugs to dull her pain. Other teens were into that stuff, but Ashlee did not feel like she was in the same place. She felt like with everything in her life she had become an adult instantly; she had no desire to do the party thing, getting drunk or high. And she did not want to follow her father to that place.

Her disbelief with everything that had happened contin-ued, and so did her anger. Ola knew that even some adults could not make it through the ongoing nightmare Ashlee had experienced—it had been so brutal. And she was still just a kid, Ola thought.

"Why me? Why?" Ashlee asked. She vented in their ses-sions, in tears. Ola let her go, let her exhaust herself by the end of each conversation. She told Ola of the guilt trip her family was now laying on her for coming forward; Ola felt the family had truly let Ashlee down. From the first time she met her, Ola could tell that all Ashlee had ever wanted was a solid family; it was everything to her, but she was clinging to something that was not there.

"You have *nothing* to feel guilty about."

She kept encouraging Ashlee, challenging her. The girl had a heart of gold, but was also tough. She had to be, Ola knew, or it all would destroy her.

"You can go through life as a victim," Ola said. "Or you can ask yourself, 'What am I prepared to do about it?'"

* * *

The living victims would forever have to cope with the dam-age left behind by Sam Pirrera, the scars never fading, and that included Sam's own extended family. His parents never commented much on their son's case. Sam's father, Antonio, did tell *The Hamilton Spectator* after the arrest: "What can I say? There's nothing to say. If he did it, he has to pay." And when Sam was charged with Bev's death, Antonio Pirrera would only say: "What I feel, I feel for me."

Sam's mother, Lina Pirrera, never commented to the media about Sam, or the case, or what she saw when she had been inside Sam's house in the wake of Maggie's murder and dismemberment, when her son finally lost it and reported to

Sam Pirrera's grave stone.

the hospital. One day, long after Sam had died, a journalist knocked on the door of the house on Cannon Street where Sam grew up, and where his parents still lived. A dark-haired young boy opened the door He looked like Sam's son. And then Lina Pirrera came to the door. She had a smooth olive-toned complexion, reddish brown hair, short and layered. The journalist asked if Lina would talk about her son.

"I don't want to talk about it," she said softly. "I just want to remember the good memories."

"Do you want to just talk about the good memories?"

Lina Pirrera's head tilted back, her face angled towards the sky, emotion starting to well in her eyes. "I want to keep the good memories for myself," she said, and slowly closed the door.

As for Sam's former home on Burns Place, it became something of a landmark for those seeking out infamous Hamilton addresses. Voyeurs rode slowly past the little house on the small court. It got to the point that a man living in the house had people knocking on his door, asking if they could look around inside and see the refurbished basement. One of the home's subsequent owners asked, and received, city permission to change the number 12 on the façade to a different number for a $130 fee.

Sam's ex-wife Danielle, meanwhile, continued to live in Hamilton in the years following his death, although she no longer went under the Pirrera name. One of the biggest "what-ifs" in the case had been, what if Danielle had come forward earlier to police with Sam's secret about killing Bev? Had she done so, and had the police run with it, Maggie Karer's life would have been saved, and other women abused by Sam spared as well. Why didn't Danielle speak up earlier? Detectives felt that Danielle either didn't believe Sam, or more likely had been abused and intimidated by him so much that she was too afraid to reveal his secret. They felt that she, too, was a victim.

She worked for a time at a Tim Hortons in the east end, at the Queenston traffic circle off Main Street East, across from the creaky old City Motor Hotel, that had once been the place to stay in Hamilton in the 1960s, and where the weathered neon sign still stood, an unkempt monument to another era. One day, in the summer of 2008, Danielle agreed to meet at the Hortons with a writer researching a book on the Pirrera case. She approached the coffee shop on foot, platinum hair, dark tan, dressed in black. In her mid-thirties, her eyes were bright and blue, but she had gained weight. She had been living on social assistance, a couple of hundred dollars a month; times had not been easy, she said. After ordering a French vanilla coffee, she got to the bottom line: she would be interviewed for the book, but only if she was paid, so that "something good comes out of something bad." The writer declined the proposal.

Danielle did say that she wanted to return to the east coast, where her current boyfriend lives. "I gotta get out of this town. Too many bad memories." She reminisced for a minute or two, about how Sam told her the first time they met she reminded him of his first wife, and that he later vowed that he would kill himself if the police ever caught him. As for her young daughter, Sam's third child, the little girl is still with Danielle, and has no idea about the case surrounding her father. "She just knows Daddy is in heaven. Even though he's not."

* * *

From the moment Lesa Davidson finally realized, much too late, that her daughter had perhaps been one of Sam Pirrera's victims, unspeakable guilt lived inside her. She had watched Bev leave her home and never return, and had failed to ask enough questions in the months and years that followed. She had been duped by Sam's lies and tricks. Bev's own mother had, in a sense, forsaken her. It ate at Lesa, and she knew that desperate feeling would never leave her.

She was not alone. Many others had fallen for Sam's big lie, one that he told often enough that it became the accepted truth. Each time Lesa might have been inclined to wonder about Bev, there was a phone call from someone claiming to be her daughter, or presents from California for the kids from Mom. How was it possible that no one thought to truly enquire where Bev had gone, to actually make contact with her? No one in Bev's family pressed Sam on it, certainly no one thought to go to the police. And no official at the family court in Hamilton pursued the issue of why it was that Beverly Davidson had all of a sudden not contested custody of her children, letting Sam file his divorce papers and take them for himself, without saying a word. (Although it is not, in fact, uncommon for a family court to issue an order of custody in the absence of one of the parties responding, even if there has been a record of past exchanges between the two.)

On one hand, Lesa could not fathom that Danielle, Sam's second wife, kept the deadly secret about Bev all those years. How could she never tell anyone? One Christmas, long after she believed Bev had left, Lesa visited the house on Burns Place, saw her grandkids, and Sam, and there was Danielle, who knew the secret but chatted with Lesa all the same, saying nothing about what she knew.

Lesa did not ultimately blame Danielle; Sam had been controlling her, too, she believed. And had Danielle revealed the secret it still wouldn't have saved Bev. And yet incredulity remained, only deepening her pain that the truth about Bev had been out there. Back when Sam Pirrera's court date had approached, Danielle had told Lesa about a dream she had when she was still with Sam. Bev had come to her in the dream. "Get out," Bev told Danielle in the dream. She thought the warning probably saved her life, pushing her to leave the man. All of which was positive for Danielle, Lesa reflected, but did not save her daughter.

Bev's Mom with photos of her daughter.

Years after it was all over, Lesa Davidson sat at the dining room table in her home in the lower city, talking about her eternal nightmare, her eyes watering with tears through a curtain of gray, as she chain-smoked through the interview. The pain of her memories caused her body to shake. Sam's death? He was a coward for taking his own life, she said, nearly spitting the words out—a coward for not facing up to what he did and explaining himself.

If she ever felt the slightest glint of triumph, it came on January 28, 2000, the day of Sam's last court appearance, when the charge of murdering Bev was announced. It was the first time Lesa had a chance to face him since his arrest, although she could not know it would be her last. Bev's mom sat in the front row, waiting for him to enter the room. She had prepared herself: do not avert your eyes; look right at him; do not flinch; do not cry. Be strong—stronger than him. Sam was led into the room in shackles. She stared at him wordlessly, tried to catch his eye. And Sam Pirrera turned and stared back at her, showing nothing in his face.

* * *

Margaret Karer, Maggie's mother, had a dream. In the dream, she is lying in bed in a dark room, and somewhere down below her, she hears voices. They grow louder, a chorus of voices, blending together. And then she can see hands reaching up around her, hundreds of hands, cold dead hands reaching up from the floor, grasping at her. And then, standing, the princess appears right in front of her in the bedroom. The princess is fresh-faced and angelic. It is her, "*Maggie, my Maggie.*" She wears a white summer dress, brushed by wind coming through a window that has no glass in it.

"I'm alive, Mom," she says.

Now Maggie walks out of the bedroom, down the hall, Mom follows her, into the kitchen, where there are two gift bags on the table, the wrapping paper glowing with reflected light. Maggie picks up the presents.

"Maggie, what is happening?"

"I'm not dead, Mom."

"He killed you."

"No. He didn't."

Margaret Karer woke up from the dream. Each time she dreamt it, she awakened to a reality she could never truly comprehend. She would see Maggie's son on occasion: he came to visit her, stayed in his mother's old room, the one where the portrait of a nameless little dark-haired girl hangs above the wood-frame bed, as it did when Maggie slept there. The son is in his 20s, by accounts a tall, dark-haired young man who is doing fine. People had tried to protect him when he was little and the news of Maggie's death broke, but life was also not easy for him. He was placed in foster care. He ran away and went to his birth father, the man nicknamed Bugsy, until police showed up and took him away and he was put back in care. Some say that, despite Maggie's high-risk lifestyle, she was a doting mother to the boy, loved him deeply, and made sure he never saw or heard anything involving her life on the street.

Photo coutesy of the author

Young Maggie and her mom.

There is not a day that goes by that Margaret Karer doesn't think about her daughter and what happened. She will never recover. The tears come easily and the disbelief has never waned. "Sometimes I say, come back, Maggie," she says in her Hungarian accent. "Please come back. I love you so much."

Like the Davidson family, the Karers had been denied so much, denied a verdict in court, or knowing precisely what happened to Maggie, and why, or even simply being able to pinpoint the day on which she actually died. Both women's memorial stones offer only general timelines to the end of their natural lives. For the families the story ends in hollow darkness. All that is left is searching hard for notions of justice, and truth, that exist beyond a courtroom, that even Sam Pirrera cannot erase.

Bev never did give up in her fight against Sam. He tried to beat her into submission but she did not quit. He lied about her; worst of all, he let her children think that she had abandoned them. But trial or no trial, the truth remained, like limestone standing as dirt and rocks crumble around it. Bev did not willingly leave her girl and boy, and in the end they knew the truth.

And Maggie, too, never surrendered. She had defensive wounds on her arms from the struggle, she fought back, just like her father, big Les Karer, would have. In that basement, in the final moment, perhaps Maggie felt the storms in her life finally calm; she passed into a different place, with no more demons, delivered from evil. She is once again just a young girl on one of those warm afternoons from long ago, lying in a friend's back yard, still a few hours until curfew; summer's not over and she has all the time in the world. Her long hair fanned out, she feels the grass against her skin. High above is sunshine and infinite blue sky, wisps of cloud, a gentle breeze kissing her cheek. She closes her eyes, yet she can see nothing but light.

# Epilogue

*Central Station*
*Hamilton, Ontario*

"Abi-Rashed." It was a woman on the phone from property section, down in the basement of Central Station. Every few months, it seemed, Peter Abi-Rashed got the call, was asked which old homicide case boxes could be transferred out of a cramped storage room down there, to a storage facility in another part of the city. He got up from his desk, walked through homicide section and downstairs to the room, the one with the concrete walls painted pale blue. He saw the eight banker-style boxes full of documents from the Pirrera case. In the years since Sam died in custody, Abi-Rashed had already overseen transport off-site of eight construction skids full of exhibits from the case—the remnants from 12 Burns Place, boxes containing pieces of broken furniture and glass, clothing, as well as most of the basement that Ident had literally stripped apart for the trial that never happened: wall paneling, carpet, pool table, the entire bar.

Exhibits and documents from closed homicide investigations are by law kept indefinitely. The Pirrera case unofficially had its own category. It was over, certainly, the only possible suspect dead. There was nothing left to pursue, although Abi-Rashed still welcomed new information on the case for the record. It was not a closed case in the strictest sense, because no one had ever been convicted for the murders of Beverly Davidson and Maggie Karer. The boxes containing evidence and witness statements that never got an airing in court were a reminder of that fact, every time the detective saw them. After working more than a hundred homicides, not much got to him, but Pirrera still touched a nerve. Pretty soon all the Pirrera boxes would be gone from the station. Abi-Rashed decided he would keep one in his own office.

Gary Yokoyama

Abi-Rashed kept a case box in his office.

Among other closed-case boxes in property section was the one for the Baby Maliek homicide that he had worked on during the Pirrera investigation. Abi-Rashed had been at the hospital when the critically injured toddler was first brought in, and the case stayed with him for a long time. In the end the investigative team pulled it off: they got them both, a double-conviction. Carlos Clarke, the boyfriend of the toddler's mother, was convicted of second-degree murder, and Maliek's mother, Carmelita Willie, of manslaughter for aiding, abetting, and failing to protect her child from Clarke. She was sentenced to seven years in a federal prison.

In another room at the station were boxes containing files from unresolved cold cases, where suspects had either not been found, or an accused not yet brought to trial. Some of them had been on Abi-Rashed's docket in the past. One was a box labeled "Short," as in Dr. Hugh Short, the Ancaster physician shot in his home in 1995, allegedly by anti-abortion killer James Charles Kopp. Abi-Rashed worked that case early on; he talked to Short in hospital the night of the shooting. Kopp remained in prison in the U.S. for murder, having been sentenced to life with no chance of parole, and it was unlikely he'd ever be forced to come to Canada to face the charge of attempted murder.

And there was the box with Clyde Frost's name on it, the 80-year-old Hamilton man whose beaten body was discovered in a van in downtown Toronto early in 1999, not long before the Pirrera case broke. Abi-Rashed shook his head about that one. They had, he believed, more than enough to prove who killed Frost. They knew who it was. The family of the victim knew it; they just needed to gather more information to meet the bar in court, where, according to the saying taped to the wall in Abi-Rashed's office, "It's not about the truth, it's the proof." He tried not to let it get under his skin. At his desk, working on something else, his eye inadvertently caught a glance of a folder icon on his computer screen bearing the name of the case. "There's Frost," he muttered to no one, and bluntly cursed.

He was one of the few officers to have stayed with Major Crime—which was ultimately renamed the Homicide Unit—

Detective-Sergeant Peter Abi-Rashed.

since the beginning, when the special branch of Hamilton's Police Service was created in 1992. He was not one to look back, but if Abi-Rashed had one regret, it was that he didn't get more years in uniform. It explained why he missed no opportunity to don the uniform at formal police functions. Working the street, on the frontline—he felt that's what being a cop was all about. In his suit and civilian car he still flagged down law-breaking motorists when necessary.

He knew homicide was where he belonged. Detectives moved out of the unit by dictate, sometimes by choice, but never stayed for too long. It is a high-intensity job, a roller coaster where you are never off the clock, the expectations are high, with families looking to you for justice, revenge. Yet the justice system sets the bar high, putting police work on trial as much as the perpetrator. Sometimes Abi-Rashed wondered what the hell he was doing still working among the merchants of misery. And yet, there is still the chase, the adrenalin rush. He had not grown tired of it. And in court, when he listened to victim-impact statements, heard families talk about the pain that does not go away, he thought, "This is why we do the job."

Pirrera? It had been perhaps his most sensational and disappointing case, a surreal experience. Nothing about it had resembled a typical homicide investigation, including its cold and brutal conclusion. And even when it was all over, he had one of the most unusual experiences he ever had on the job, one that, for a rare moment, made him nervous. It was the day he got a call from Sam's teenage daughter. Ashlee Pirrera wanted to meet him face to face and learn the truth.

* * *

For a time she had stopped wanting to live at all, in the wake of so much death and abuse in her life. Ashlee made it through, in part thanks to the counsel of her social worker Ola Furda, who had been like a second mother, and also with the help of people like Father Mark Sullivan from her church, and a teacher named Julie Angiolillo. Ola called it a "circle of acceptance" for Ashlee, after having faced so much rejection in her young life.

Ola also tried to help Ashlee find closure regarding the death of her mother. When Ashlee was still at St. Jean de Brebeuf Catholic Secondary School in Hamilton, Ola dropped by to pick her up for lunch as she often did. As it happened, there was a boy in Ashlee's grade with whom she shared a terrible common link—Maggie Karer's son. The two students knew of each other at school, but never formally met.

On this day, after lunch Ola drove Ashlee to the White Chapel Memorial Gardens. It had been a couple of years before that she had been forced to stay away from the service for Bev. But Ola learned from the police where the small memorial stone lay, and now she led Ashlee to the spot. Ashlee was happy, and sad, to see the symbolic grave in her mother's name.

She moved on, through high school and into a program in social work at Mohawk College in Hamilton, where she wanted to study to help abused kids. But she would soon discover that she had not escaped her past, or the feeling of being trapped by it. And there were still questions that nagged her. She had read bits and pieces of articles about her father, but continued to hear her family deny much of what had been reported. She wanted answers about what her father had really done. Ola Furda agreed that it was time for her to get them. She showed Ashlee all of the articles that she had saved about Sam Pirrera. And still, Ashlee had more questions, but about things that only the police could answer. One day, Ashlee, who was 17 at the time, called the detective who had played a large role in putting away her father. Peter Abi-Rashed agreed to meet her.

It was a rare moment on the job that the hardened homicide investigator felt anxious. "What am I walking into?"
Abi-Rashed wondered. He even felt more apprehension than
he would notifying a next of kin of a death during an investigation. He knew all about that part of the job, but he had
never met with the child of a killer he had helped put in jail.
And he was also acutely aware that his pursuit of the second
murder charge against Sam Pirrera, for Bev's death, had perhaps pushed the man over the edge to suicide. For all this, he
expected young Ashlee Pirrera to lay into him.

But when they sat in a room together, within two minutes
he knew it would be a calm discussion. He was impressed.
After all she had been through, he thought, Ashlee had grown
into a self-assured and articulate young woman, mature beyond her years, who asked smart questions. He told her what
she wanted to know, the basics of what Sam had done to Bev,
and Maggie, and what went on at Burns Place the day Sam
unraveled and was checked into the hospital. He tried not to
get too graphic but gave it to her as straight as possible. He
got the sense Ashlee knew the basics of what had happened
already and just wanted it verified, after being shielded from
reality by her family for so long. He also told her how he had
known Sam on the streets when Abi-Rashed was a young
cop, how Sam ran with troublemakers in the east end, but
that he would have never predicted Sam would come to lead
the life he did.

While Ashlee was outwardly composed, she felt very
nervous at the meeting, having waited for this moment for so
long. She had mentally come to a place where she didn't think
she cared what the police had to say, good or bad; she just
wanted the truth. When she heard what Abi-Rashed told her,
she was sad and angry and emotional, but kept it together and
felt relieved in a way. She felt like she could truly try to move
on. She also felt more hard feelings towards her grandma, Lina
Pirrera, after hearing what Abi-Rashed had to say.

"I haven't looked at my grandma the same way since. Nor have I looked at the police system the same way ... how do you get away with something like that?"

Even with everything she now knew, Ashlee was not prepared for what appeared in *The Hamilton Spectator* two years later, when she was 19 years old—a 13-part series on the Pirrera story. When the series launched, her younger brother, who was 15, phoned Ashlee in hysterics about it. A reporter from the *Spectator* had told Lina Pirrera that the series was coming, but she did not warn the kids. Ashlee worked at McDonalds, her co-workers knew her last name, and they put it together. Most didn't say anything, others asked questions, some were less than sensitive, wondering aloud if she would go crazy one day like her father.

"You don't understand," Ashlee told them, "my dad was an addict; it's not in my *blood*."

She was bitter about the exposure. She met with Ola Furda, who told her it was perhaps a sign that she had not adequately dealt with it all yet. By the end of the series, after reading and learning more about her mother in the newspaper, Ashlee felt differently. The story had been a good thing, therapeutic in a way. Eventually she even asked her boyfriend to read the series so that he would better understand her. It also reunited her with her Nana, Bev's mother, Lesa Davidson. Ashlee had not spoken to her in years, because her grandma had discouraged contact with Bev's side of the family. Ashlee now rediscovered her Nana, and Lesa Davidson regained her granddaughter.

She continued to try and cultivate a relationship with her mom in her head and heart, even as it was often painful and frustrating. She was only able to barely remember Bev; she had been with her mom less than four years. But then, some say the first months of a life are critical, setting the stage for an individual's development. Ashlee spent most of this time with Bev, more so than any other person. And ultimately she grew into a feisty and resilient young woman, against the odds, just like her mom had been. It was this toughness that had surely kept Ashlee alive and sane through a protracted nightmare that would have ruined most people. "All that time she spent with Bev was so important," Ola said. "Her mother did something right."

* * *

*British Columbia*
*Spring, 2008*

In the morning she woke in the apartment, rose, and looked into the faces of her deceased parents. One of the pictures on her dresser showed smiling 18-year-old Bev Davidson, and standing beside her, shorter, in a jean jacket, shadow beard, was 20-year-old Sam Pirrera, holding their baby—Ashlee, crying.

Ashlee was now a few months away from turning 21. She had, in a physical sense, escaped her past, left cold and grey Hamilton on a miserable winter day for the warmer, cedar-tinged air and frost-tipped mountains on Canada's west coast, to be with her boyfriend, Ryan. The relationship started out as a friendship back in Hamilton, but when Ryan left for B.C., it turned into a long-distance romance. And then, in February 2008 Ashlee decided it was time to leave the city where she had always lived, and her doctor agreed that getting away was a good idea.

Before she left, she talked with Ola. She was nervous for Ashlee, wondered if she would make it, leaving for a boy. But from what she heard, Ryan seemed like a solid person, had an apprenticeship, and by accounts a good family. A fresh start was something Ash needed, to get away from the bad memories. Ryan visited Hamilton. Ashlee joined him on the return trip, and she stayed out west.

And then Ashlee decided to do something that she had been thinking about for a long time—formally changing her last name from Pirrera to Davidson. She knew it would not endear her to her grandmother. She heard Lina Pirrera once tell her that changing her name would not change who she was. But Ashlee no longer wanted to be associated with the Pirrera name. And, in fact, she knew that the day she was born, her birth certificate had read Davidson. It had simply evolved into Pirrera over the years when her mother was thought to have abandoned her, and Ashlee was too young to have any say in the matter. But no longer.

Moving to the other side of the country helped her start over, but sorting through her emotions and memories remained a gradual process. Her feelings about her father continued to be complicated. He had done such horrible things, but she believed it was his addiction that created the monster. She wondered if Sam's upbringing had a negative impact on his future actions, cultivating crack cocaine personality and rage. She remembered that he had his moments as a decent father, and felt that in his core he had the potential to be a good person. He would always be her father, and she could not exist without him. At the same time she hated him for taking away her mother and killing Maggie. Some things you simply can't forgive.

She continued to have a recurring dream about him: Ashlee is back in Hamilton's east end, on Madison Street, which ran right behind her mom's childhood home on Adams. She is drawn towards a house, walks in through an open door. It is pitch black inside, but she sees a coffin, its lid open, empty. And then Sam Pirrera appears from out of the darkness in the hall and chases her. Ashlee makes it out of the house every time, but her dad does not; he is somehow trapped, unable to leave. The dream ends with the house catching fire. Then it is engulfed in flames, but it does not collapse—it just keeps burning.

Out west, not yet 21 years old, Ashlee became pregnant. It thrilled her. She was a young mother, certainly, although not as young as her mom had been. Now she could build her own family with Ryan. It gave Ashlee a new focus where she could channel her nurturing. Her Nana was excited about the news, even her grandma sounded pleased. Ashlee told Ola the

Ashlee Davidson started a new life out west.

news, said that she and Ryan planned to get married at some point after the baby was born, and would Ola attend the event? Years ago young Ashlee had made Ola promise she would come to her wedding some day. Ola confirmed, she would not miss it. Ashlee e-mailed her a photo, showing the defined baby bump, a proud smile on the heart-shaped face.

On Mother's Day 2008, as often happens on birthdays and other milestone days, she awoke with emotion building inside her. Ashlee thinks about Bev all the time, wonders if somewhere her mom can see her, if she's proud of how far she has come, if she feels sadness for not being here. She wonders if her mom is like a guardian angel to her. For all these questions, Ashlee is not sure of the answers, but she does not stop asking.

Beside her bed she keeps a small album of photos Nana gave her of Bev. A couple of times a week, it depends on if she's stressed about something, or even the weather, it can be anything that prompts her, she opens it up. On this morning, she did not open the album. Whenever she felt her emotions bubbling over, she had this feeling of being trapped, of needing to escape. And so she put on her iPod and went outside for a walk, listened to a soothing instrumental called "Kisses and Cake," and she cried. Later, she was able to crack the album. One of the images is of the two of them, just baby Ashlee and Bev. Mom is in a bathrobe, her hair golden, kissing the baby girl's little foot, both of them soaking in the moment, glowing. It is Ashlee's favorite. She doesn't know much about the picture, when it was taken, where it is set, but she knows enough.

"She just looks like she loves me a lot."

POST-
MORTEM

JUSTICE AT LAST
FOR YVETTE BUDRAM

JON WELLS

ISBN: 978-0-470-15547-9

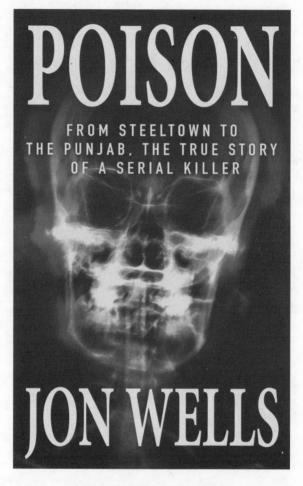

# POISON

## FROM STEELTOWN TO THE PUNJAB, THE TRUE STORY OF A SERIAL KILLER

# JON WELLS

ISBN: 978-0-470-15548-6

ISBN: 978-0-470-15546-2